Building
Real
Intimacy

MARRIAGE

Interactions Small Group Series

Authenticity: Being Honest with God and Others
Character: Reclaiming Six Endangered Qualities
Commitment: Developing Deeper Devotion to Christ
Community: Building Relationships within God's Family
Essential Christianity: Practical Steps for Spiritual Growth
Fruit of the Spirit: Living the Supernatural Life
Getting a Grip: Finding Balance in Your Daily Life
Jesus: Seeing Him More Clearly
Lessons on Love: Building Deeper Relationships
Living in God's Power: Finding God's Strength for Life's Challenges
Love in Action: Experiencing the Joy of Serving
Marriage: Building Real Intimacy
Meeting God: Psalms for the Highs and Lows of Life
New Identity: Discovering Who You Are in Christ
Parenting: How to Raise Spiritually Healthy Kids
Prayer: Opening Your Heart to God
Reaching Out: Sharing God's Love Naturally
The Real Deal: Discover the Rewards of Authentic Relationships
Significance: Understanding God's Purpose for Your Life
Transformation: Letting God Change You from the Inside Out

InterActions
small group series

Building
Real
Intimacy

MARRIAGE

BILL HYBELS

WITH KEVIN AND SHERRY HARNEY

ZONDERVAN™

GRAND RAPIDS, MICHIGAN 49530 USA

WILLOW
Willow Creek Resources

ZONDERVAN™

Marriage
Copyright © 1996 by Willow Creek Association

Requests for information should be addressed to:

Zondervan, *Grand Rapids, Michigan 49530*

ISBN-10: 0-310-26589-4
ISBN-13: 978-0-310-26589-4

Interior design by Rick Devon and Michelle Espinoza

Printed in the United States of America

08 09 10 11 12 /❖ DCI/ 10 9 8 7

CONTENTS

INTERACTIONS

In 1992, Willow Creek Community Church, in partnership with Zondervan and the Willow Creek Association, released a curriculum for small groups entitled the Walking with God series. In just three years, almost a half million copies of these small group study guides were being used in churches around the world. The phenomenal response to this curriculum affirmed the need for relevant and biblical small group materials.

At the writing of this curriculum, there are nearly 3,000 small groups meeting regularly within the structure of Willow Creek Community Church. We believe this number will increase as we continue to place a central value on small groups. Many other churches throughout the world are growing in their commitment to small group ministries as well, so the need for resources is increasing.

In response to this great need, the Interactions small group series has been developed. Willow Creek Association and Zondervan have joined together to create a whole new approach to small group materials. These discussion guides are meant to challenge group members to a deeper level of sharing, to create lines of accountability, to move followers of Christ into action, and to help group members become fully devoted followers of Christ.

SUGGESTIONS FOR INDIVIDUAL STUDY

1. Begin each session with prayer. Ask God to help you understand the passage and to apply it to your life.
2. A good modern translation, such as the New International Version, the New American Standard Bible, or the New Revised Standard Version, will give you the most help. Questions in this guide are based on the New International Version.
3. Read and reread the passage(s). You must know what the passage says before you can understand what it means and how it applies to you.
4. Write your answers in the spaces provided in the study guide. This will help you to express clearly your understanding of the passage.
5. Keep a Bible dictionary handy. Use it to look up unfamiliar words, names, or places.

SUGGESTIONS FOR GROUP STUDY

1. Come to the session prepared. Careful preparation will greatly enrich your time in group discussion.
2. Be willing to join in the discussion. The leader of the group will not be lecturing, but will encourage people to discuss what they have learned in the passage. Plan to share what God has taught you in your individual study.
3. Stick to the passage being studied. Base your answers on the verses being discussed rather than on outside authorities such as commentaries or your favorite author or speaker.
4. Try to be sensitive to the other members of the group. Listen attentively when they speak, and be affirming whenever you can. This will encourage more hesitant members of the group to participate.
5. Be careful not to dominate the discussion. By all means participate! But allow others to have equal time.
6. If you are the discussion leader, you will find additional suggestions and helpful ideas in the leader's notes.

ADDITIONAL RESOURCES AND TEACHING MATERIALS

At the end of this study guide you will find a collection of resources and teaching materials to help you in your growth as a follower of Christ. You will also find resources that will help your church develop and build fully devoted followers of Christ.

Introduction: Building Real Intimacy

"You're driving too fast for road conditions."

"I've got it under control."

Our voices cut sharply above the speeding click of the windshield wipers.

For hours the sleet had pounded the windshield. For hours we had sat in bitter silence.

Thank God for the darkness. Thank God the kids slept quietly in the back of our blue and gray Suburban. Thank God we were almost home.

It should have been a wonderful Christmas vacation. Our Washington, D.C., accommodations, reserved and paid for by a generous friend, were comfortable and roomy. The kids, feeling very grown-up at eleven (Shauna) and eight (Todd), enjoyed the freedom to roam alone through the huge old hotel that was nearly deserted because of the holidays; they were delighted to let Mom and Dad sleep in while they went downstairs to order breakfast on their own. Our tourist schedule was relaxed and modified to meet the kids' desires: their ideal afternoon balanced two hours at the Smithsonian with two hours in the hotel pool. Historic Georgetown was within walking distance, and each evening we strolled by the windows of quaint shops and chose from an assortment of curious eateries. One evening, while the boys "cruised" the town, the girls laughed and cried through Dickens' *A Christmas Carol* at the Ford Theater. Sounds wonderful, doesn't it?

For the kids it was—we hope. We did our best to create a memorable experience for them. But for us it was a dreadful week. Pleasant accommodations and a carefully planned itinerary could not ease the pain of our troubled marriage. The inviting king-sized bed in our private room could not bridge the gap between estrangement and intimacy. Frustration, loneliness, hopelessness, fear, despair, and grief overshadowed every potential joy and defied every attempt to break through them. While the kids roamed, we talked, but every conversation drove us further apart. We became increasingly dissatisfied with ourselves and angry at one another. We felt trapped, as we had so often in the past. Our commitments to the children, to the church, and to God kept us clinging to a marriage that all too often broke our hearts.

We drove into our driveway on the first day of the new year. Happy New Year.

Now, contrast this story with another scene.

"I've never seen so many stars."

"It's like a black velvet dome studded with diamonds."

Lazy waves eased slowly up the sandy beach, then rolled back into the dark ocean waters. We lay on our backs on the sand, dreamy from the hypnotic rhythm of the gentle seas. There was not a hint of chill in the night air. Ah, to be cradled in creation.

The only thing that matched the perfection of that night was the day that had preceded it. We had awakened to a drizzly dawn, sipped lemon tea in our tiny rented cottage, then walked the beach toward the rainbow that arched in the south. The colors brightened while we watched, then faded as the morning sun sucked the moisture from the air. We walked waist deep in the water, then dove beneath the shimmering surface. We swam till our muscles ached, then let the buoyant swells carry us back toward shore. Tiny, silver slips of fish skimmed the surface of the water beside us, then flashed and dove and chased in an underwater playground of conches and clams and moon shells. Refreshed by our swim, we showered the salt from our hair, then dressed for the day in appropriate vacation attire—another swimsuit. We ate a late breakfast of granola and fruit, then each grabbed a book, scrunched sand and beach towels into chairlike mounds, and aimed our sunscreened faces toward the south.

The weather, with its cloudless sky, was at its best; and more importantly, we were at our best. The days of unrushed living had softened our rough edges and mellowed our intensities. We spoke softly and laughed easily. We traded books back and forth, insisting that the other read the "wonderful passages" we had just read. We compared notes and insights. We reminisced and talked of the future. We revealed fears and acknowledged foibles and discussed dreams and shared secrets. And the pleasure of that day gave way to romance beneath the stars.

Despair in the front seat of a Chevy Suburban? Or romance under a diamond sky? Which describes the real Hybels' marriage?

They both do. In fact, those two real-life episodes occurred within months of one another. It hardly seems possible, yet bouncing between those dramatic contrasts has been the pattern of our relationship since we met at seventeen. Our highs have been heartthrobbingly wonderful; our lows have been devastating. During the highs we think that meeting one another was the best thing that ever happened to us; during the lows we rue the day our paths crossed.

In this series of six sessions you will have opportunities to honestly look at your marriage and identify areas of strength as well as areas you need to grow. Whether you are in a stormy time in your marriage or experiencing inexpressible bliss, this series of interactions will help you build real intimacy with your marriage partner.

Bill Hybels

LEARNING FROM HISTORY

It was the summer of 1974, and Lynne and I had been married two months. She informed me that the garbage disposal had quit working. I told her to call a repairman.

The war was on!

"What do you mean, call a repairman? Why pay fifty dollars for a job any able-bodied man can do?"

"Well, you don't expect *me* to do it, do you? I don't know anything about garbage disposals. I'd probably electrocute myself if I touched it. Besides, we're short on butter knives."

"You could do it if you tried. You just don't care enough."

The problem was that Lynne's dad fixed things, her brother fixed things, her uncles fixed things, her cousins fixed things, and so she assumed that *all* men fixed things. Unless, of course, they weren't interested in what was going on at home. Unless they were too preoccupied with concerns outside the home to devote thirty minutes to household needs.

From my side, I had never had a successful experience with anything mechanical in my life. I knew I would waste hours and probably money if I tried to fix the garbage disposal or anything else. I also believed, as my father had, that the sensible approach was to stick with what I was good at and pay someone else to do what I wasn't good at.

A WIDE ANGLE VIEW

1 Tell a story about a time you and your spouse discovered how differently you approach things.

A BIBLICAL PORTRAIT

Read Genesis 2:21–25 and Ephesians 5:31–33

2 Both of these passages present three critical steps in the marriage process. What does it mean to:

- Leave our father and mother

- Be united to our spouse

- Become one flesh

SHARPENING THE FOCUS

Read Snapshot "The Powers That Shape Us"

THE POWERS THAT SHAPE US

Lynne and I now realize that who our fathers and mothers were, how they related, and how our families operated played a *major role* in shaping us as individuals. This is true for everyone. Two decades spent in close proximity with a single group of people can't help but shape our personal identities. We are who we are largely because of the experiences we have enjoyed—or endured—within the context of our unique family units.

Family dynamics determine our self-esteem and self-confidence. Family values shape our character. Family experiences influence our concepts of how marriage should be structured and how children should be raised, of how we should view work, recreation, education, money, politics, and religion. We all look at our families and decide either to repeat the pattern if our experience was basically positive, or try to create an opposite situation if our experience was basically negative. Either way, we are profoundly affected by the attitudes and actions of our families.

3

How did your parents handle:

- Conflict

- Expression of emotions

- Celebration of special occasions such as birthdays, holidays . . .

- Family vacations

- Discipline of children

4 Cite at least one difference in your personalities that
can be traced directly back to your family backgrounds. How has this become an issue in your marriage, and how are you seeking to deal with it?

5 What aspects of your parents' relationship do you
respect and want to see imitated in your own
marriage?

What are you doing to develop these in your relationship?

Read Snapshot "No One's Perfect"

NO ONE'S PERFECT

Sadly, there are more to family memories than highlights. In addition to being one of the greatest determiners of personal identity, the family is also one of the greatest causes of personal pain. No one grows up pain free. The apostle Paul tells us that no one can live a totally righteous life (Rom. 3:23), and that includes parents. There is no perfect mom. No perfect dad. We are all products of parents who were sinners. They too were products of parents who were sinners, just as our children will be. We must realize that imperfect parents always cause some degree of pain to their children. The baton that is passed from one generation to the next is always at least a little disfigured, a little scarred.

---

6 What is one characteristic that marked your parents' relationship that you want to avoid in your marriage?

What would it require for you to confront and avoid these same patterns?

7 How could you creatively thank or affirm your parents for the positive ways they have impacted your life?

Looking Back Together

Take time in the coming week to talk with your spouse about an incident in your past where one or both of your parents did something that wounded you. Discuss the following questions:

Could it have been avoided?
How have you recovered?
Are there steps you need to take to continue the healing process?
How do you plan to keep from repeating the same mistake in *your* family life?

Take time to pray for healing in the heart of your spouse and commit to continue praying for them in the days and weeks to come. Also, take specific steps toward continuing the healing process in your lives.

Research Project

Call or meet with one of your in-laws and ask them how they feel their life has impacted your spouse. Give them freedom to talk about their positive and negative influence. Follow this up by telling your spouse what you learned. Take time to affirm your in-laws, honoring them as people who matter to you and to God.

HOW ARE YOU WIRED?

REFLECTIONS FROM SESSION 1

1. If you took time with your spouse to reflect back on some of the struggle and pain they faced growing up, what did you learn about how you can care for your spouse in your relationship now? If you are still in the healing process, how can your group help you to walk through this healing process with courage and hope?

2. If you contacted one of your in-laws, what did you learn about your spouse through this conversation? How can you use what you learned to more effectively love and support your marriage partner?

THE BIG PICTURE

Almost every person who walks a wedding aisle comes to a point in the development of the marriage relationship when he or she says, "I think I made a terrible mistake. I think I married the wrong person."

Often people in the throes of fear and confusion say things like this: "I don't feel like I know my spouse anymore. We had so much in common while we were dating, but now we seem to see everything differently. This isn't the person I fell in love with. My spouse has changed so much."

Actually, your spouse has probably changed very little. But reality often reveals what romance conceals. In the day-to-day routine of real life spouses begin to notice things they hadn't seen before. They tend to focus on their differences rather than on the common beliefs or interests that drew them together. They tend to become irritated by the idiosyncrasies that charmed them when they were dating, and they tend to look at the negative side of the very qualities they most admired in one another before they were married.

I see this pattern in many marriages. As a matter of fact, it is all too evident in mine. During our courtship, our feelings flourished in the rich soil of our obvious compatibility. We held in common our deepest values and our highest goals. We respected one another. We enjoyed an intense whole-person attraction for one another. Our problem was that we focused all our attention on these delightful points of contact and neglected to pay attention to some important points of difference. We didn't look at the differences in our family backgrounds discussed in the previous lesson, or the differences in our basic personalities.

A WIDE ANGLE VIEW

1 What are some of the common beliefs and interests that first drew you to your spouse?

2 What is one difference between you and your spouse that you did not discover until after you were married? What are some of the consequences of this difference?

A BIBLICAL PORTRAIT

Read 2 Corinthians 6:14–18

3 This passage says, "Do not be yoked together with unbelievers." What implications does this have on the union between fully devoted followers of Christ and non-Christians?

SHARPENING THE FOCUS

Read Snapshot "Introverts and Extroverts"

INTROVERTS AND EXTROVERTS

Introverts think before they speak and usually say little. They prefer a few close friends rather than many acquaintances, and would often opt for a quiet night at home rather than a social get-together. They may be warm, caring, and friendly toward people, but social interaction drains them (they feel slightly uncomfortable in groups), so they need a heavy balance of energizing solitude. They need to get alone where they can relax, "let down," and be themselves again.

Extroverts, on the other hand, derive energy from interaction with people. Most extroverts enjoy working and playing on a team. They usually have many friends and spend much of their time with others. Extreme extroverts love nothing more than a party—and usually end up being the life of it. They tend to talk a lot; in fact, it sometimes seems they have to talk in order to figure out what they think. Extroverts enjoy solitude now and then, but too much of it drains them emotionally. They need the inspiration of interaction to keep their batteries charged.

---

4 After reading the definitions above, take a moment to write down which one you feel describes you and your spouse. Use this simple rating, 1 being mild and 10 being extreme, to judge where each of you "lands" on the continuum. This same rating system will be used on questions 5–7. (This will be fun. For example, you might say you are a very strong introvert, but your spouse may think you are only a mild introvert!)

Person	Introvert or Extrovert	Rating
Me:	_____	_____
My Spouse:	_____	_____

How do your self-evaluations compare with your spouse's evaluations?

How do these differences in personality reveal themselves in day-to-day life?

How can awareness of these differences help you get along better with each other?

Read Snapshot "Sensers and Intuitives"

SENSERS AND INTUITIVES

If *sensers* were to describe themselves in one word, it would probably be "practical." Sensing people tend to base their reality on facts, facts, and more facts. They have their feet firmly planted in reality. Giving little thought to what might have been or what may be in the future, they focus on what really happened or what is. They look to the past, learn through experience, and highly value other people's experiences. When "sensing" employers interview potential employees, they tend to focus questions on the applicants' history, reasoning that past experience is the best basis for assuming future productivity.

Intuitives would probably describe themselves as "innovative." For them, what *is* can always be improved upon. Their vague sense of dissatisfaction with reality propels them toward change. The future intrigues them far more than the past or present, and they are fascinated with ideas and possibilities. Intuitive employers interviewing prospective employees tend to pay more attention to what the applicant says regarding the future of the organization than what he or she has done in the past. Intuitives delight others with their speculation, imagination, creativity, and poetic imagery, but because their heads are often in the clouds, they are subject to error regarding facts and details.

5

After reading the definitions above, take a moment to write down which one you feel describes you and your spouse. Use the same rating system as described in question 4 (1 being mild and 10 being extreme).

Person	Senser or Intuitive	Rating
Me:	_____	_____
My Spouse:	_____	_____

How do your self-evaluations compare with your spouse's evaluations?

How do these differences in personality reveal themselves in day-to-day life?

How can awareness of these differences help you get along better with each other?

Read Snapshot "Thinkers and Feelers"

THINKERS AND FEELERS

A third category—that of thinkers and feelers—shows how people differ in the area of assessing choices and making decisions. *Thinkers* take a logical approach to life, preferring to let their heads rule. They tend to be cool and calculated, cut-and-dried. They concern themselves with right and wrong, with prudence, with goals, with efficiency. In the legal system, they cry for justice; in business, for productivity and profit; in education, for unwavering truth. If something is right, they do it. If something is fair, they promote it. If something makes sense, they pursue it.

Feelers prefer to let their hearts rule. They feel deeply themselves and empathize easily with how others feel. They tend to base their decisions on how their choices will affect others. They hate it when people feel sad or hurt or discouraged, and long to be able to ease their pain. They prefer mercy over justice, put people ahead of profits, and sometimes see gray where thinkers see black and white.

6

After reading the definitions above, take a moment to write down which one you feel describes you and your spouse. Use the same rating system as described in question 4 (1 being mild and 10 being extreme).

Person	Thinker or Feeler	Rating
Me:	_____	_____
My Spouse:	_____	_____

How do your self-evaluations compare with your spouse's evaluations?

How do these differences in personality reveal themselves in day-to-day life?

How can awareness of these differences help you get along better with each other?

Read Snapshot "Initiators and Responders"

INITIATORS AND RESPONDERS

Initiators create ideas and action. They are aggressive, assertive, and willing to confront. They tend to be outspoken, often talking loudly and quickly, adding emphasis with intonation and body language. Initiators make decisions easily, and express them with directness and intensity. They know how to take charge and like to do it. They can be excellent leaders, though they sometimes seem overwhelming to others.

Responders prefer to let other people's ideas and actions come their way. They are less assertive and aggressive than initiators and avoid confrontations whenever possible. They are indecisive and cautious, and tend to speak quietly and unemotionally, hesitating to express their opinions for fear of imposing them on others. They listen carefully, avoid the use of power if at all possible, and have a generally supportive attitude. Others view them as shy, but likable.

7 After reading the definitions above, take a moment to write down which one you feel describes you and your spouse. Use the same rating system as described in question 4 (1 being mild and 10 being extreme).

Person	Initiator or Responder	Rating
Me:	_____	_____
My Spouse:	_____	_____

How do your self-evaluations compare with your spouse's evaluations?

How do these differences in personality reveal themselves in day-to-day life?

How can awareness of these differences help you get along better with each other?

8

Explain to your group how your deeper understanding of personality differences will help strengthen your marriage. How might learning about others in your group help all of you build deeper community and authentic relationships?

PUTTING YOURSELF IN THE PICTURE

FINDING COMMON GROUND

In this session you discussed some of the common beliefs and interests you had that originally attracted you to your spouse. Identify one or two of these points of common interest from those early days and discuss what you can do to pursue these interests today. How can you get back to some of the root beliefs and interests that first drew you to each other?

Also, identify any new interests the two of you have in common. What can you do to spend time pursuing one of these interests together in the coming month?

SEEING THINGS FROM WHERE I STAND

Identify the area in this session, (e.g., Introvert vs. Extrovert) where you and your spouse are the farthest apart. Take time to explain to your spouse why you think you are wired the way you are. Be sure to affirm your spouse for who they are. There are no good or bad personality types—just different ones. Reflect on how you can celebrate those differences.

PLANNING FOR PEACE

REFLECTIONS FROM SESSION 2

1. What is an area of common interest that you and your spouse are enjoying together at this time? What have you done in the past few weeks to spend more meaningful time together?
2. If you took time as a couple to identify the area in your personalities where you are least alike, tell the group what you learned about each other in this process and how you are seeking to affirm one another, celebrating each other's unique God-given design.

THE BIG PICTURE

Some time ago, when Lynne and I were still dating, we sat down to talk with a couple who absolutely amazed us. They had dated for three years and had *never* had a single fight. They were confident this pattern would continue.

Then they asked us, "What about you two? You've been dating for a long time. What's it been like for you?" We were more than a little intimidated. How could we sit across the table from this "perfect" couple and spill the truth about our stormy romance and our broken engagement? Would it hurt to "soften" the story a bit?

We responded, "Oh, we've had a few conflicts. But nothing major, and we've always been able to resolve them. Besides, we think it's healthy for dating couples to "go at it" now and then and learn to work things out. What better way to prepare for marriage?"

They remained confident and said, "Well, maybe that's true for you. But if we could make it through three years of dating without a problem, I don't see why we should expect trouble in marriage. We won't have the pressures of college, or living with our parents, or juggling part-time jobs. Marriage should be easy compared to what we're dealing with now. It'll be a snap."

We wished them well and left the restaurant thinking that maybe they were right. Maybe marriage *would* be a snap for them. Maybe they could maintain their perfect record. They sure seemed like an ideal match.

But we—and they—were wrong. Establishing careers, maintaining a home, and just living with one another proved to be a bigger challenge than our friends had anticipated. They couldn't figure out how to divide household responsibilities. They discovered they had opposing perspectives on money. In-law tensions put them at odds. Colliding schedules caused frequent angry explosions. Sexual frustrations kept them awake at night. They couldn't agree on vacation plans. . . .

And they desperately needed a vacation! They needed an escape from reality. After three years of marriage, they felt imprisoned by a solid wall of conflicts they did not know how to resolve. And inside the wall, the air was steaming with the heat of hostility.

A WIDE ANGLE VIEW

1 What would you say to an engaged couple who claimed to never fight and who were confident this pattern would continue for their whole marriage?

Tell a little about your courtship and dating experiences. Was this time in your relationship smooth sailing or rough seas?

A BIBLICAL PORTRAIT

Read Ephesians 4:25–26

2 Why is speaking the truth so critical for healthy relationships?

Reflect back on a time when you failed to "speak the truth." What consequences did you experience?

3 The apostle Paul does not say anger is wrong. However, he does warn us about sin that can come from anger. He says clearly, "Do not let the sun go down while you are still angry." Why is following this teaching essential for a healthy marriage?

How can refusing to follow God's teaching on how to handle anger, and instead, just "keeping it inside," give the devil a foothold?

SHARPENING THE FOCUS

Read Snapshot "What We Learned"

WHAT WE LEARNED

Our style of fighting and the way we deal with conflict often mirrors what we saw in our home as we grew up. There are a variety of ways we can respond during times of conflict in our marriages. Here are just a few:

Freeze 'Em Out. This style of handling conflict leaves everyone cold. No one wants to talk about real issues or concerns so everyone backs off, detached, and holds their hurt and anger inside. This leads to withdrawal from relationship.

Let the Bullets Fly. In this cowboy style of conflict, everyone squares off and starts shooting verbal bullets. Intimidation is the tool used in this style. Feelings are expressed with anger and feelings are hurt. A great deal of damage is done.

Let Me Out of Here. This style is all about running. It can take various forms: a trip to the bar, to the shopping mall, home to parents, drugs, workaholism, or anything else that creates a temporary escape. However, when the person returns, the problem remains.

I Don't Know What Happened. Sadly, some people explode and express their anger with physical violence. A verbal assault escalates to a physical attack. Afterward, the one who exploded will often say, "I don't know what happened." But the damage is already done. These and many other unhealthy patterns can mark marriage relationships. We need to learn to identify what we learned in our home growing up and develop healthy ways to deal with conflict.

---

4 How did your parents deal with conflict and anger in their relationship?

How do you deal with conflict and anger in your marriage?

Read Snapshot "The Spirit of Reconciliation"

THE SPIRIT OF RECONCILIATION

We have observed that in addition to knowing practical tools for conflict resolution, nearly all couples who survive the minor and major conflicts of married life have discovered a key antidote for marital demise. It is called *the spirit of reconciliation*. This elixir produces a heart condition that predisposes people toward reconciliation and revolutionizes the way they approach conflict.

There are three steps in this process of reconciliation:

First, we need to acknowledge we have fallen short of the moral standards of our holy God and that we are therefore in conflict with Him.

Second, we must understand that God, "being rich in mercy," offered His Son, Jesus Christ, to bring us back to God.

Third, when we realize we have been adopted into God's family even though we don't deserve it, a joy of divine reconciliation begins to naturally overflow into every area of our lives, including our marriage.

---

5 Why are the first two steps of this process necessary for the third to become a reality in our lives?

If you have taken the first two steps in your life, have you taken the third step? If so, describe the results. If not, what stands in the way of pursuing reconciliation in your relational life?

Read Snapshot "Is That a Plank in Your Eye?"

IS THAT A PLANK IN YOUR EYE?

In the Sermon on the Mount Jesus challenged His followers to point their fingers at themselves before pointing them at others. "Why," He asked, "do you look at the speck of sawdust in your brother's eye and pay no attention to the plank in your own eye? How can you say to your brother, 'Let me take the speck out of your eye,' when all the time there is a plank in your own eye? You hypocrite, first take the plank out of your own eye, and then you will see clearly to remove the speck from your brother's eye" (Matt. 7:3–5).

What does this say to spouses? It tells us that every time we feel slighted, offended, taken advantage of, or hurt, before we take out the guns and start shooting—or running away or freezing someone out—we need to get alone with God and ask some probing questions. *Am I the problem here? Am I being unreasonable or selfish or insensitive? Am I*

---

6 Take a few minutes on your own to pray, asking God to help you see specific areas in your marriage where you might be creating problems or tension because there is sin in your life. What "planks" do you see in your eye at this time in your marriage?

Take a few minutes to break into couples and honestly confess where you know you have brought pain or hurt to your marriage. What can you do to make things right?

Read Snapshot "Can We Talk?"

CAN WE TALK?

Paul's words about not letting our anger build up suggest daily peace talks for conflicts that have arisen in the course of that day. Busy schedules sometimes make that impossible, and serious issues may require more formally scheduled peace talks, but even those should be scheduled as soon as possible. In the meantime, couples must covenant together not to "sin in their anger." They must both refrain from the kind of "cheap shots"—sarcasm, innuendo, and rudeness—that inevitably complicate the issues.

As you enter into discussion to resolve conflict and tension in your relationship, there are a number of very important guidelines:

Prepare with prayer. It is essential to pray for a tender heart and humility in this process.

Begin with affirmation. Be sure you verbally express your love and commitment to your spouse.

Be willing to take blame. You must be ready to acknowledge specifically how you have contributed to tension in your marriage.

Express hurt, not hostility. Communicate your hurt honestly but not in anger.

Make direct statements. Hints and offhand remarks accomplish little. Say what you mean.

Make "I feel" statements. Don't accuse and antagonize by placing blame on your spouse. Tell them how you feel. "I feel lonely," is better than "You're never home."

Avoid "never" and "always" statements. Seek to be accurate, truthful, and realistic in what you say. Don't say, "You never come home on time," but say, "I feel sad (or hurt) when you are late."

---

7 This may be a stretch for your marriage. How do you feel about taking the risks to engage in an honest, truth-telling relationship in your marriage?

8 How can your small group function as a place where you can gain counsel, advice, and accountability for your marriage?

PUTTING YOURSELF IN THE PICTURE

SETTING GROUND RULES

Take time as a couple to set ground rules for how you will conduct your peace talks. Consider these ground rules to be a covenant. You may want to use the sample covenant below as a starting point for your discussion.

1. We will always pray as we begin to talk about any concerns.
2. We will seek to come to this time with a spirit of reconciliation.
3. We will be willing to look at where we have fallen short in the relationship and try to see the plank in our own eye.
4. We will always begin with affirmation of our love for each other and our commitment to our marriage.
5. We will seek to express our hurt but not hostility.
6. We will seek to communicate clearly and make direct statements.
7. We will seek to express feelings rather than assign blame.
8. We will avoid "never" and "always" statements.
9. We will seek the support and help of committed Christian friends as needed.

10. _____

11. _____

12. _____

We commit to follow these guidelines as we grow in communication and see peace in our marriage relationship.

Signed: _____ and _____

COMMIT TO MEMORY

Take time in the coming days to memorize this passage:

"In your anger do not sin": Do not let the sun go down while you are still angry (Eph. 4:26).

WHATEVER HAPPENED TO ROMANCE?

REFLECTIONS FROM SESSION 3

1. If you signed a covenant for how you will handle peace talks as a couple, tell your group about the agreement you have made together. What can your group do to keep you accountable to your agreement with your spouse?

2. If you took time to memorize Ephesians 4:26, how has this verse impacted your attitude since you have committed it to memory? How does having God's Word in your mind and heart help you live more effectively as a follower of Jesus Christ?

THE BIG PICTURE

"We need to get the romance back." I have heard so many spouses make that statement. Couples who are unhappy with their marriages often admit that what disturbs them more than anything is the lack of romance. "If I married the right person," a spouse asks, "why did the courtship end so abruptly after the wedding? Why did the flames die so quickly? Why is there so much less "feeling" in our marriage than there used to be?"

Few couples expect to maintain the intense, supercharged, adolescent-style relationship that marked the height of their courtship. In fact, most couples feel somewhat relieved when life begins to settle into a more normal routine and they can get about the tasks of real life again. But many marriages settle down too much. Within a few short years the sparkle has faded completely. Feelings have become mere memories. Romance has become something to read about in cheap novels. Spouses relate like roommates who share an occasional one-night stand. And together they face many more years of disappointment and frustration.

A WIDE ANGLE VIEW

1 Take a moment on your own to rate the romance factor during the following times of your relationship with your spouse. Rate each one from one to ten: (10 being strong romantic feelings and expressions and 1 being virtually no romantic feelings or expressions).

Time in your relationship	*Rating:*
During the first year we dated	_____
During our engagement	_____
During our first year of marriage	_____
At the present	_____

What factors have contributed to the changes in your ratings?

What feelings arise as you view these changes? (Sadness, surprise, disappointment, excitement?)

A BIBLICAL PORTRAIT

Read Song of Songs 4

2 This book of the Bible is one of the greatest love songs ever written. It expresses a depth of romance, intimacy, and friendship that most of us only dream of having in a marriage. What kind of feelings do you experience when you read this passage?

3 How do you think God feels about romantic and passionate love between a husband and wife?

SHARPENING THE FOCUS

Read Snapshot "Romance Busters"

ROMANCE BUSTERS

There are many things that can drain the romance and excitement out of marriage. Here are a few that many couples deal with:

The curse of familiarity. Sadly, we often pamper and care for new things: cars, homes, clothes, and even relationships. But with time, we don't exercise the same care and concern. Familiarity breeds laziness, and we no longer take the time to nurture our spouse.

A twisted sense of security. Sometimes marriage partners work hard during the courtship phase of a relationship, but now they feel they have their prize and no longer need to work at the relationship—it's secure!

Physical exhaustion. Let's face it, often we simply feel too tired to put a lot of energy and creativity into our marriage. While dating, couples would stay up talking until 2:00 A.M. Now it's hard to stay up past 10:00 P.M.

Too many responsibilities. Schedules are full to the point of overload. Children, careers, church, community, and personal responsibilities fill our schedules, and we just don't have time to be together like we used to.

Financial burdens. Mortgages, car payments, raising children, and a list of other expenses can weigh us down and make it tough to be as creative in our dating as we were during those early days. Money tensions often mean marriage tensions.

4 Take a moment to reflect and respond to each of the "Romance Busters" listed below. How many of these are you experiencing in your life and marriage right now?

Romance Busters

Is this a factor in your marriage at this time?

- Feeling things have become too familiar

  ___ Very much so
  ___ Some
  ___ Not at all

- Feeling oversecure

  ___ Very much so
  ___ Some
  ___ Not at all

- Physical exhaustion

  ___ Very much so
  ___ Some
  ___ Not at all

- Too many responsibilities

  ___ Very much so
  ___ Some
  ___ Not at all

- Financial burdens too familiar

  ___ Very much so
  ___ Some
  ___ Not at all

What are some other "Romance Busters" you have experienced?

5 If you had to honestly answer "very much so" to two or three of the items on the "Romance Buster" list, don't be surprised if you are not experiencing the most romantically intense time in your marriage. If you answered "very much so" to four or five items on the list, you are probably not experiencing much romance *at all* in your relationship.

What can you do to get some of these items off your list and move toward a more romantic marriage relationship?

Read Snapshot "Shifting Gears"

SHIFTING GEARS

 I have to be honest here and say that I am addressing the men more than the women at this point in our session. Some marriages have lost their romance because a woman has had her worst nightmare come true. She married a man who swept her off her feet with tender words, flowers, romantic dinners, and late-night strolls along the beach. She thought it would always be like this. Now he hardly communicates, never buys flowers, falls asleep in front of the TV, and no longer seems too interested in late-night walks. The man she married is gone. What happened?

I fear that too many of us men approach marriage like a job to get done. Once we have our bride, all the courtship stuff goes out the window: manners, flowers, love poems, and nice dinners. They were just part of the chase.

This change in husbands often leaves wives confused and even resentful. This can also happen the other way. Some men watch their wives change after the wedding day and feel the same kinds of resentment.

---

6 Take a few minutes to pray and reflect on the following questions:

What were some of the things I did during our courtship and engagement that I stopped doing after we got married?

What promises did I make to my spouse before we got married that I have failed to follow through on after we were married?

If I have wronged my spouse in either of these ways, what can I do to make it right?

7

Take time as a couple to discuss the following:

If you "shifted gears" after you got married and feel you might have hurt your spouse in the process, take time to admit that you recognize your mistake and let your spouse know you are sorry.

If you have not followed through on promises made to your spouse, what are you going to do to make this right and be a person of your word?

8 What new commitments have you made to each other that you would feel comfortable telling the group about? Sharing commitments with others will foster healthy accountability and allow others to support you with prayer and encouragement.

Ask your group to encourage you, support you, and keep you accountable as you seek to follow through on these commitments.

PUTTING YOURSELF IN THE PICTURE

MY BEST TIME

Busy schedules and physical exhaustion can take the romance out of a marriage. Talk as a couple about which day of the week and what time in the day each of you would say is your "best time." When do you feel fresh, sharp, and the most energized? Try to plan a date or time together in the coming week that will reflect giving each other the best of your time. You might be surprised at what a positive impact this has on your time together.

THE GOOD OL' DAYS

Often financial tensions can stand in the way of romance. Some couples avoid dating because of the cost. Sit down as a couple and make a list of at least five things you can do on a date for ten dollars or less. Schedule two of these things in the coming month and follow through on them.

FANNING THE FLAMES OF MARRIAGE

REFLECTIONS FROM SESSION 4

1. What would you say is your best time in the course of your day and your week? When are you the freshest and at your best? What are you doing to give some of your best time to your spouse and the building up of your marriage?

2. If you have taken your spouse on a creative and inexpensive date recently, tell your group members about it so they can grow in creativity in their dating life.

THE BIG PICTURE

On a Wednesday evening in May of 1989 Lynne and I loaded our luggage into our car and began a journey to a destination where we would spend our fifteenth wedding anniversary. After more than three hours on the road and a stop at an all-night restaurant for dessert, we ended up on the beach in South Haven. This was the very place we went on our first date a decade and a half earlier.

There was the same concrete breaker upon which we had sat. The same lighthouse under which we had talked. The same moon whose beauty we had admired. It was 3 A.M. We sat on the beach, digging our toes into the sand, watching the moon-lit waves shimmy up the sodden bank. With each wave came a memory that crashed into our consciousness. A memory of a slammed door and a canceled courtship. Of making up and of a carnival wedding. A memory of joy surrounding a baby's birth and of tears shed in a cracker-box home. Memories of criticism and of judgment and of celebrating uniqueness. Memories of feelings smothered by pain and of rekindled romance.

We were seventeen when we first sat together on that Lake Michigan beach—and naive. We foresaw only sunny days. By thirty-seven our naiveté had been battered and finally destroyed by rainstorms and lightning and gale-force winds. But while our naiveté had not survived, we had. We had come face-to-face with reality, and we had stared it down. We had persevered and worked hard and won. We sat on that beach stronger and more mature and more tolerant and more in love than ever.

A WIDE ANGLE VIEW

1 As you look back on your courtship and marriage, what are some of the moments you remember with fondness? What are some of the experiences and struggles you are thankful to have made it through?

A BIBLICAL PORTRAIT

Read 1 Corinthians 7:3–5

2 What does this passage teach about sexual expression in the marriage relationship?

3 The apostle Paul says that after a couple has been apart for a time, they should "come together again." One reason for this exhortation is so that they will not be tempted by Satan. What problems and temptations can a couple face when they refrain from sexual intimacy for prolonged periods of time?

When is it appropriate for a couple to abstain from sexual intimacy?

SHARPENING THE FOCUS

Read Snapshot "Talk, Talk, Talk"

TALK, TALK, TALK

Feelings grow best out of conversation, so that is where we need to start. Couples must devote themselves to talking—about anything, everything, important things, mundane things, pleasant things, disturbing things. Romance begins with knowledge of one another, and the key to knowledge is open, honest, consistent communication.

Is it any wonder we lose the warmth in our relationships when we only talk on the run, when we leave each other memos on the kitchen table and messages on the answering machine? Too often spouses don't feel love for one another anymore because they don't *know* one another anymore. They don't know each other's fears or dreams or goals or disappointments or plans. They don't know what goes on during each other's day. They aren't aware of the joys, the stresses, the responsibilities, the successes that fill their spouse's world. The truth is, the flame of marriage begins to die down when we stop talking.

---

4 When are some of the times in your day or week that you and your spouse naturally find time to talk together?

What topics tend to dominate your conversations?

What can you do to spend more time talking together?

Read Snapshot "Don't Bury the Hurt"

DON'T BURY THE HURT

If the romance in your marriage has received a near-deadly blow, your conversations will undoubtedly have to begin by focusing on hidden hostilities. If you are like Lynne and me, you are probably tempted to bypass this and move to more pleasant conversations. "The past is past," you say. "Let's forget it and move into the future." But that doesn't work. Underground hurts will undermine even your most earnest attempts to rebuild romance, and you will end up more frustrated than when you started.

It is unrealistic to expect negative emotions that have built up over a number of years to dissipate in one conversation. People who have been deeply hurt need to give themselves the freedom to constructively express their hurt over and over again if necessary. Those who caused the pain need to listen patiently, understanding that while working through past hurts can be painful and sometimes seem counterproductive, it is *essential* to rebuilding romance.

5
Why is it critical to deal with hurt feelings and talk about them rather than try to bury them?

Read Snapshot "Court Creatively"

COURT CREATIVELY

After you get rid of hidden hostilities and learn what it means to talk again, you can begin to court creatively. Most couples put the wedding gifts away and their courting days behind them. But if you want to rebuild romance you need to court again. Fortunately, courting is like riding a bike; you may get a little rusty, but you never forget how.

Here are just a few suggestions about how you can begin to court your spouse again:

- Write your spouse a short love letter reminding them how much they mean to you.

- Call your spouse during the day for the single purpose of saying "I love you!"

- Communicate love with nonsexual touching: a hug, a kiss, a backrub, or just holding hands with no expectations of further intimacy.

- Give unexpected gifts: flowers, candy, or anything that would touch their heart.

- Make time to date. Be creative and go out together regularly.

- Find opportunities to serve each other. What can you do to help lift the load your spouse bears each day?

- Encourage and inspire your spouse. Everyone should know you are your mate's fan.

6

Tell about one of the most memorable dates you and your spouse have had.

Which of the items listed in the Snapshot above would most communicate love to you and why?

Read Snapshot "Language of Love"

LANGUAGE OF LOVE

For some people *touch* is the primary language of love. Their spouse can say "I love you" twenty times a day and prove it through countless acts of kindness, but without an embrace or a kiss or a squeeze they won't *feel* loved. Other people need to hear *verbal expressions* of love. They need to hear in concrete terms why their spouse loves them. "I'm glad I married you because . . ." assures them that their spouse recognizes and appreciates their individuality. *Service* is another thing that makes some people feel most loved. These people respond best to affection that is revealed in practical terms: cooking a meal, mowing the lawn, repairing a faucet, running an errand, helping with a distasteful chore. They see acts of service as indicative of what is in their spouse's heart. *Gifts* make still other people feel loved—not because of the cost involved, but because of the personal attention and thought that goes into them. These people enjoy—even need—*tangible* reminders of their spouse's love. Finally, *spending time together* makes other people feel loved. They don't care particularly what they and their spouses do, as long as they are together. Having their husband or wife commit uninterrupted blocks of time to them assures them they are top priority. The key is to learn what says "I love you" to your spouse and speak it loudly, clearly, and often.

7

What is it that speaks the language of love to you? How does it feel to hear that language?

What do you think speaks the language of love most clearly to your spouse?

What can you do in the coming days to speak the language of love loudly and clearly to your spouse?

PUTTING YOURSELF IN THE PICTURE

CREATIVE DATING

In the coming month, have each of you plan an evening out. Set a dollar amount you are going to limit yourselves to and then be creative. The person planning the date should let their spouse know what time to be ready and how to dress (casual or formal). As you plan the date, think creative, think romantic, and think about your spouse.

LEARNING TO TALK AND LEARNING TO LISTEN

So often couples get to talk only on the run or in brief fragmented sections of time between all the business of life. Block out two hour-long sections of time to be together in the coming weeks. Pick prime time when both of you will be fresh and energetic. Designate each time for one of you to guide the conversation. All this means is that you get to pick what you talk about during the hour. Both of you need to agree to stick to the topic chosen by the designated leader of the conversation. Be ready with good questions that will open the door for meaningful discussion together.

LIVING IN CRISIS MODE

REFLECTIONS FROM SESSION 5

1. If you have been trying to develop a habit of dating your spouse and making sure you get out on a regular basis (this means just the two of you with no kids), how has this commitment to regular dating impacted your relationship?

2. If you took time to block out two periods of time for directed conversation and listening as outlined at the end of your last session, what did you learn about your communication style? What did you learn about your spouse's style of communication?

THE BIG PICTURE

It was a Saturday morning in December a few years ago. I went to my office early to finish the sermon I had to give that evening at church. At 5:30 A.M. I was on page twelve of my message. By 1:30 P.M. I was on page eight. I was in big trouble.

To complicate matters, I had to do a wedding before five hundred people that afternoon, and I hadn't given one thought to what I was going to say to the young couple and their gathered family and friends. I thought about my unfinished message, about the wedding, and about the evening church service, and in a moment of total frustration, I laid my head down on my desk and cried.

Almost before the first teardrop hit the desk I reminded myself that falling apart was a ridiculous waste of time, and I quickly mopped myself up. But in that brief moment of "losing it" I had seen the truth: The wheels were coming off my carefully constructed wagon.

That fall our church had added another weekly service, which meant that I taught Wednesday, Thursday, and Saturday nights, and twice on Sunday morning. In between message preparation and actual teaching, I squeezed in an increasing load of administrative duties and travel commitments. I had thought I was up to the challenge of an increased teaching schedule, and I had charged into the autumn months prepared to run the kingdom race as hard and as fast as I'd ever run it before. But all of a sudden, it seemed I couldn't run at all.

I hobbled through the fall, hanging on till Christmas vacation. I left with my family for what was supposed to be a quiet family retreat. Through unforeseen events, we ended up instead in a hotel mob scene. It was the kind of place where you had to wait twenty minutes for an elevator, and when the elevator came it was so crowded you couldn't get in. That was the last straw. I was in a mild state of frenzy the entire week.

When we got home I went alone to Wisconsin for three days to recuperate, think, and pray. "God, what's happening to me? I don't understand what's going on in my life, but I feel like I'm going under. Help me."

I spent the following year putting the pieces of my life back together. By delegating certain ministry responsibilities I was able to continue working, but at a greatly reduced pace. The remainder of my time I devoted to personal healing and to some long-overdue reflection on the pattern of life that had finally driven me to the breaking point.

A WIDE ANGLE VIEW

1 Tell about a time in your life when you felt your schedule and life were so busy that you had to slow down or you feared you would burn out.

What can you do about your schedule to slow down the pace of your life at this time in your life?

A BIBLICAL PORTRAIT

Read Psalm 46

2   What picture does this psalm paint of what life can be like?

According to this psalm, how can followers of Christ find peace and calm in the midst of the storm?

3   This psalm talks about troubles, the earth giving way, mountains falling, nations in an uproar, and other signs of turmoil and stress. What are some of the things in your life and schedule at this time that make your life stressful?

What do you do that contributes to that stress?

SHARPENING THE FOCUS

Read Snapshot "Pegged in the Red"

PEGGED IN THE RED

Crisis-mode living is when you spend every waking moment of every day trying to figure out how to keep all of the balls in the air and all of the plates spinning. In crisis mode you keep running faster and faster, from project to project, deadline to deadline, quota to quota, meeting to meeting, event to event, practice to practice. Your RPMs keep creeping higher and higher until you hit the red line.

Most active people have to spend a certain amount of time in crisis mode. Life just turns out that way. You're an accountant and it's tax season. You repair air conditioners and it's August in Phoenix. You're cramming to take the bar exam. Your kids are breaking out with chicken pox. You have two weeks to meet a sales quota.

The problem arises when you spend too much time in crisis mode. That's when crisis mode goes from being a season of life to becoming a way of life. When that happens—when you keep the needle pegged in the red week after week, month after month—you start doing the only thing you can do. You economize. You shortchange your investment of energy in certain areas of your life so you can invest it in other areas—usually in the performance-oriented areas to which your self-esteem is tied. Nothing matters but keeping those all-important balls in the air and those ultimately significant plates spinning, so you use all your energy accomplishing those feats. In every other area of life, you become a miser; you hoard your energy, you engage minimally, you touch superficially, you slide along the surface, you *skim*.

4

What are some of the potential consequences of keeping the RPMs of your life pegged in the red for too long?

- In your spiritual life

- In your relationships with your spouse and with your children

- In your physical health

- In your emotional health

Read Snapshot "A Shrinking Heart"

A SHRINKING HEART

The emotional depletion that results from living in crisis mode eventually produces a *shrinking heart*. This is a heart that does not worship as authentically as it once did or love God as passionately as it used to. It is a heart that is no longer sensitive to the needs of others, a heart that has lost the fire of compassion.

While the hearts of healthy Christians keep enlarging to encompass more of the heart of Christ, the hearts of Christians in crisis mode become shriveled and weak. A man from our church said, "You're right about the crisis mode. I have a bigger staff, a bigger budget, a bigger building, a bigger house, and a bigger bank account than I had five years ago. And all I have to show for it is a hollow cavern where my heart used to be."

5 How have you seen your heart shrink and grow hard during times you have stayed in a crisis mode for too long?

How did this affect your marriage?

What helped you turn this around and grow more tender-hearted again?

Read Snapshot "Opt for a Slow Charge"

OPT FOR A SLOW CHARGE

If you were to go out in your garage and turn on every accessory in your car, you could probably drain the battery in about five minutes. To recharge it, you would have two choices. First, there is the quick charge. This is a fast-acting method that gets cars running in record time, but if used frequently it burns out the plates in the battery. Second, there is the method all responsible mechanics suggest: the trickle charge. With this approach, it takes six to eight hours to get a battery recharged to full strength, but it doesn't burn out the plates. It replaces the lost energy *and* preserves the life of the battery.

Drained *emotional* batteries need a trickle charge too. A trickle charge involves determining what replenishes you emotionally and then incorporating that into your schedule. It also means spacing your emotionally draining responsibilities in such a way that in between them you can trickle charge back up to emotional fullness. In our culture that is no small challenge.

6

What recharges your batteries and brings freshness to your life?

What can you do in the coming month to incorporate more of this into your lifestyle?

7

What tends to drain your batteries and leave you depleted?

How can you take some of these things out of your schedule in the coming month?

Read Snapshot "Dare to Downshift"

DARE TO DOWNSHIFT

Are your emotional batteries low? Has your heart shrunk? Has the love drained out of your relationships? Do you think you might be heading for a crash?

If you are living in crisis mode, Beware. It *will* catch up with you, and it *will* undermine your marriage and family life. So please, don't rush from one emotionally draining activity to the next. Don't live so fast that you never have time for replenishing recreation or relationships. Don't neglect your need to trickle charge.

Perhaps you, too, need to make some radical changes in your life. Maybe you need to revise your job description. Or cut down on travel commitments. Maybe you need to resign from that board or drop that extra class. Another answer may be to refuse to take on so many projects, or hire some extra help, or downscale your goals. You may even have to take a demotion or say no to a wonderful opportunity—or a whole fistful of opportunities. How good, after all, is an opportunity that throws you into crisis mode? How great is a lifestyle that never gives you time to enjoy life?

8

If you are living in a crisis mode at this time, or if you sense you are heading toward a crisis mode, what specific things can you do to downshift before things get worse?

As a group, commit to support one another in crisis mode, holding each other accountable to make wise choices and set appropriate lifestyle priorities.

PUTTING YOURSELF IN THE PICTURE

HELPING YOUR SPOUSE RECHARGE THEIR BATTERY

Take time in the coming week to ask your spouse to list five things you can do to help lift their burdens and recharge their battery. List those in the space below and set personal goals to work at one or more of these in the coming month.

Take time in the coming week and ask your spouse to gently, but honestly, list three things you do that can deplete their battery. List those in the space below and set personal goals to work at not doing these things in the coming month.

LEADER'S NOTES

Leading a Bible discussion—especially for the first time—can make you feel both nervous and excited. If you are nervous, realize that you are in good company. Many biblical leaders, such as Moses, Joshua, and the apostle Paul, felt nervous and inadequate to lead others (see, for example, 1 Corinthians 2:3). Yet God's grace was sufficient for them, just as it will be for you.

Some excitement is also natural. Your leadership is a gift to the others in the group. Keep in mind, however, that other group members also share responsibility for the group. Your role is simply to stimulate discussion by asking questions and encouraging people to respond. The suggestions listed below can help you to be an effective leader.

PREPARING TO LEAD

1. Ask God to help you understand and apply the passage to your own life. Unless that happens, you will not be prepared to lead others.
2. Carefully work through each question in the study guide. Meditate and reflect on the passage as you formulate your answers.
3. Familiarize yourself with the leader's notes for each session. These will help you understand the purpose of the session and will provide valuable information about the questions in the session.
4. Pray for the various members of the group. Ask God to use these sessions to make you better disciples of Jesus Christ.
5. Before the first session, make sure each person has a study guide. Encourage them to prepare beforehand for each session.

LEADING THE SESSION

1. Begin the session on time. If people realize that the session begins on schedule, they will work harder to arrive on time.
2. At the beginning of your first time together, explain that these sessions are designed to be discussions, not lectures. Encourage everyone to participate, but realize some may be hesitant to speak during the first few sessions.

3. Don't be afraid of silence. People in the group may need time to think before responding.

4. Avoid answering your own questions. If necessary, rephrase a question until it is clearly understood. Even an eager group will quickly become passive and silent if they think the leader will do most of the talking.

5. Encourage more than one answer to each question. Ask, "What do the rest of you think?" or "Anyone else?" until several people have had a chance to respond.

6. Try to be affirming whenever possible. Let people know you appreciate their insights into the passage.

7. Never reject an answer. If it is clearly wrong, ask, "Which verse led you to that conclusion?" Or let the group handle the problem by asking them what they think about the question.

8. Avoid going off on tangents. If people wander off course, gently bring them back to the passage being considered.

9. Conclude your time together with conversational prayer. Ask God to help you apply those things that you learned in the session.

10. End on time. This will be easier if you control the pace of the discussion by not spending too much time on some questions or too little on others.

We encourage all small group leaders to use *Leading Life-Changing Small Groups* (Zondervan) by Bill Donahue while leading their group. Developed and used by Willow Creek Community Church, this guide is an excellent resource for training and equipping followers of Christ to effectively lead small groups. It includes valuable information on how to utilize fun and creative relationship-building exercises for your group; how to plan your meeting; how to share the leadership load by identifying, developing, and working with an "apprentice leader"; and how to find creative ways to do group prayer. In addition, the book includes material and tips on handling potential conflicts and difficult personalities, forming group covenants, inviting new members, improving listening skills, studying the Bible, and much more. Using *Leading Life-Changing Small Groups* will help you create a group that members love to be a part of.

Now let's discuss the different elements of this small group study guide and how to use them for the session portion of your group meeting.

THE BIG PICTURE

Each session will begin with a short story or overview of the session theme. This is called "The Big Picture" because it introduces the central theme of the session. You will need to read this section as a group or have group members read it on their own before discussion begins. Here are three ways you can approach this section of the small group session:

- As the group leader, read this section out loud for the whole group and then move into the questions in the next section, "A Wide Angle View." (You might read the first week, but then use the other two options below to encourage group involvement.)
- Ask a group member to volunteer to read this section for the group. This allows another group member to participate. It is best to ask someone in advance to give them time to read over the section before reading it to the group. It is also good to ask someone to volunteer, and not to assign this task. Some people do not feel comfortable reading in front of a group. After a group member has read this section out loud, move into the discussion questions.
- Allow time at the beginning of the group for each person to read this section silently. If you do this, be sure to allow enough time for everyone to finish reading so they can think about what they've read and be ready for meaningful discussion.

A WIDE ANGLE VIEW

This section includes one or more questions that move the group into a general discussion of the session topic. These questions are designed to help group members begin discussing the topic in an open and honest manner. Once the topic of the session has been established, move on to the Bible passage for the session.

A BIBLICAL PORTRAIT

This portion of the session includes a Scripture reading and one or more questions that help group members see how the theme of the session is rooted and based in biblical teaching. The Scripture reading can be handled just like "The Big Picture" section: You can read it for the group, have a group member read it, or allow time for silent reading. Make sure everyone has a Bible or that you have Bibles available for those who need them. Once you have read the passage, ask the question(s) in this section so that group members can dig into the truth of the Bible.

SHARPENING THE FOCUS

The majority of the discussion questions for the session are in this section. These questions are practical and help group members apply biblical teaching to their daily lives.

SNAPSHOTS

The "Snapshots" in each session help prepare group members for discussion. These anecdotes give additional insight to the topic being discussed. Each "Snapshot" should be read at a designated point in the session. This is clearly marked in the session as well as in the leader's notes. Again, follow the same format as you do with "The Big Picture" section and the "Biblical Portrait" section: Either you read the anecdote, have a group member volunteer to read, or provide time for silent reading. However you approach this section, you will find these anecdotes very helpful in triggering lively dialogue and moving discussion in a meaningful direction.

PUTTING YOURSELF IN THE PICTURE

Here's where you roll up your sleeves and put the truth into action. This portion is very practical and action-oriented. At the end of each session there will be suggestions for one or two ways group members can put what they've just learned into practice. Review the action goals at the end of each session and challenge group members to work on one or more of them in the coming week.

You will find follow-up questions for the "Putting Yourself in the Picture" section at the beginning of the next week's session. Starting with the second week, there will be time set aside at the beginning of the session to look back and talk about how you have tried to apply God's Word in your life since your last time together.

PRAYER

You will want to open and close your small group with a time of prayer. Occasionally, there will be specific direction within a session for how you can do this. Most of the time, however, you will need to decide the best place to stop and pray. You may want to pray or have a group member volunteer to begin the session with a prayer. Or you might want to read "The Big Picture" and discuss the "Wide Angle View" questions before opening in prayer. In some cases, it might be best to open in prayer after you have read the Bible passage. You need to decide where you feel an opening prayer best fits for your group.

When opening in prayer, think in terms of the session theme and pray for group members (including yourself) to be responsive to the truth of Scripture and the working of the Holy Spirit. If you have seekers in your group (people investigating

Christianity but not yet believers) be sensitive to your expectations for group prayer. Seekers may not yet be ready to take part in group prayer.

Be sure to close your group with a time of prayer as well. One option is for you to pray for the entire group. Or you might allow time for group members to offer audible prayers that others can agree with in their hearts. Another approach would be to allow a time of silence for one-on-one prayers with God and then to close this time with a simple "Amen."

LEARNING FROM HISTORY

GENESIS 2:21—25, EPHESIANS 5:31—33

INTRODUCTION

Like it or not, our parents have had a powerful impact on our lives. Our behavior patterns, opinions, attitudes, and faith often reflect what we learned in the home where we were raised. In this first study we will look at our family history and see how we have been influenced by our parents. Our goals will be, first, to learn all we can from the strengths in our parents' relationship and, second, to learn about the pitfalls they may have fallen into along the way, so that we do not follow in the same path.

THE BIG PICTURE

Take time to read this introduction with the group. There are suggestions for how this can be done in the beginning of the leader's section.

A WIDE ANGLE VIEW

Question One When Lynne and I look back on the story in the beginning of this study, we realize we were both out of line. Because Lynne's dad was so unusually capable in this area, Lynne had very unrealistic expectations of me. There was no way I could possibly have pleased her; I simply did not have the right skills. Also, she had always viewed her father's household help as an act of love, and wrongly interpreted my unwillingness to try to fix things as an indication that I didn't care about our home life. For my part, because my dad didn't repair anything around the house, I wouldn't repair anything either—even things I really could have fixed. And, because Lynne handled our finances, she knew that more often than not we couldn't afford a repairman. So, either the things wouldn't get fixed, or she would have to fix them herself. Actually, Lynne was pretty good at fixing things, but because of my workaholism, she was already handling more than her share of household responsibilities; she didn't want to have to be Mrs. Fix-it, too.

It took us a long time to get to the bottom of our extreme positions. We could have avoided a lot of conflict and frustration if we had talked through this issue before we got married. It would have helped me to know that Lynne's dad built televisions and houses and cars in his spare time. And it would have helped Lynne to know that my dad didn't know which end of the hose to hold to wash a car. Perhaps we would have adjusted our expectations accordingly.

While household repairs created a problem, they were nothing compared to the travel issue. Shortly before our first anniversary I announced that I was going on a vacation.

"Oh, great, where are we going?"

"No, you don't understand. I said *I* am going on vacation."

"Not without me you're not."

I couldn't believe her attitude. Why was she being so possessive and clingy and insecure and stubborn and selfish? What was her problem? Was she afraid to let me out of her sight? Did she think we had to do *everything* together? There was no way I was going to back down on this one. My dad used to call my mom from the airport and inform her that he was going to South Africa for five weeks. Why shouldn't I enjoy the same freedom?

But when I took off by myself (even for a few days) Lynne was convinced that I didn't love her. "Don't you like to be with me?" she asked. "Are you trying to get away from me?" Her father disliked spending even one night away from her mother. She couldn't understand why I sought the freedom of occasionally being on my own.

Eventually we settled into a pattern that we both enjoy—a pattern somewhere between the extremes of our parents. In fact, we've even flip-flopped some. Lynne frequently enjoys going off by herself, while I often find myself urging her to join me on trips. But we could have avoided a lot of hurt and misunderstanding in the early years if we had discovered this differing perspective while we were dating and had agreed on a compromise before the wedding.

A BIBLICAL PORTRAIT

Read Genesis 2:21–25 and Ephesians 5:31–33

Question Two Allow time for group members to interact and communicate what they feel each of these statements means. Each one has a distinct and important meaning.

- *Leave our father and mother.* This deals with the process of separation. When we get married, clear lines of separation from the homes of origin are essential. This does not mean we stop having meaningful relationships with our parents. However, it does mean we form a new home and a new family unit. There can be many problems if the leaving process does not happen and parents still control our lives and decisions.
- *Be united to our spouse.* This is the process of the union of a man and woman before God. We experience a real and life-changing effect when we say, "I do!" We no longer function as a single person; we are bound to our spouse for life. This is a joy and also a deep responsibility. The Bible talks about covenants or agreements. These spiritual contracts mean a great deal to God, and they should be taken seriously by us.
- *Become one flesh.* This language is intimate. It deals with the spiritual reality that goes along with the physical intimacy of marriage. Once we are married, God looks on the expression of sexual intimacy as beautiful and part of His perfect plan. When a husband and wife join together in sexual, "one-flesh" intimacy, not only do their two bodies become one, but a spiritual oneness occurs.

SHARPENING THE FOCUS

Read Snapshot "The Powers That Shape Us" before Question 3

Question Three Don't plan on discussing all of these. Allow group members to pick which ones they want to talk about. You may find some common ground, but you may also be surprised how differently marriage partners' parents raised them. The goal here is to allow some of these differences to begin to surface.

Question Five Do you want to learn more about your spouse? Then talk in depth about your respective families. Talk about your mom and dad's personalities, their strengths and weaknesses, their talents and abilities, their hobbies, their jobs, their friendships. Talk about their marriage. Look at how they related to one another, expressed love, resolved conflicts, made decisions. Look at how they handled finances and divided household responsibilities and disciplined their children.

Describe the atmosphere of your home. Talk about how emotions were handled. Examine the values that held priority in your family and the behaviors that were rewarded. Describe the house you grew up in, and discuss your family's standard of living. Discuss the forms of recreation your family enjoyed and your favorite family vacations. Share the experiences that shaped your self-esteem and built your self-confidence.

Tell how holidays and birthdays were celebrated. Discuss gift-giving practices. Tell what it was like to be sick when you were a child. Describe a typical mealtime conversation. Recall bedtime routines. List the chores you were responsible for. Reflect on how you related to grandparents, aunts and uncles, cousins.

In addition to promoting mutual understanding, such conversations can spark hopes and shape dreams for the future. Pleasant memories and treasured traditions can provide building blocks upon which a couple can build their own marriage and family life.

Read Snapshot "No One's Perfect" before Question 6

Question Six While it is important to talk about family highlights, it is even more crucial to discuss the lowlights. The problems. The painful memories. The disappointments. The things you hope will never be repeated in your own home.

A discussion of lowlights may be one of the most difficult and unnatural conversations a couple can have. Most of us have an overwhelming urge to defend the families we grew up in. We feel disloyal and guilty when we reveal negative family dynamics to outsiders. It helps to remember that every family— even the best of them—has a shadow side. And every young man and woman has some degree of pain, some little disappointment, some slight scar that remains long after he or she has left the family home. Those things must be discussed because they always—*always*—produce some kind of backlash. And the deeper the problem, the fiercer the backlash.

A friend of ours grew up in an extremely hostile home. His father was a tyrant who ordered his kids around and slapped them into submission. On the surface, the kids cowered in fear; underneath, they seethed with anger. They were never allowed to verbalize either the fear or the anger. Five years into marriage, our friend's wife was shocked by a sudden change in her husband. He became distant, stubborn, rebellious.

They went to a counselor and discovered that the fear and anger that had poisoned his youth were making their inevitable claim on his adult life. Together they worked through it, but it wasn't easy.

A woman we know was frustrated by her lack of sexual desire for her husband. She loved and respected him, found him physically attractive, and desperately wanted to experience true sexual oneness with him. But she could never offer more than a physical response; her inner feelings never matched her actions. Finally she went to a counselor and uncovered a story of sexual abuse. She had never been raped, but repeated episodes of inappropriate touching by a family member had left their mark. To avoid the emotional pain of the abuse, she had learned to shut down her sexual feelings; years later, in each intimate encounter with her husband, her feelings shut down automatically. Awakening them took her on a long and painful journey.

Another woman we know was a sincere and growing Christian, but she never felt as though she measured up to God's expectations. She never felt as if she was serving enough, or praying enough, or giving enough, or growing enough. So she pushed herself until she became chronically overscheduled, stressed-out, negative, and unhappy. Through the help of a Christian counselor, she realized that her frame of mind was destroying her relationship with her husband. Her problem was one that afflicts many devout Christians. She had grown up in a rigid, legalistic environment and viewed God as a commanding officer issuing long lists of harsh orders and withholding praise from all but the most intense. Hers was a God one could fear, but hardly love. This counselor convinced her that the demanding God of her parents was not the giving God of Scripture. Eventually she dropped her burdens, learned to love God freely from a joyous heart, and began to serve in healthy, constructive ways. Her husband rejoiced in the changes her new outlook produced in their marriage.

What is the common point of these diverse examples? The shadow sides of our family experiences—whether they involve false values, mistaken beliefs, harsh behaviors, abuses, mis-understandings, or disappointments—profoundly affect us as adults and marriage partners. It is imperative, therefore, that we share with one another the downside, that we ask and answer the tough questions. What are your most painful childhood memories? What was your biggest disappointment? Did you ever feel unloved or neglected? Was there emotional, physical, or sexual abuse in your home? Were either of your parents alcoholics? Were your parents divorced?

The obvious benefit of answering these questions is that it helps partners understand one another better. Another benefit is that sometimes it helps partners understand *themselves* better. Openly discussing our past with someone with whom we feel safe and comfortable often helps us discover things about ourselves—sometimes unpleasant or unhealthy things—that we hadn't been aware of before. Once the problems come out into the open, they can be dealt with so they won't come back to haunt the marriage later on.

Question Seven Allow group members to identify practical ways they can communicate affirmation and thankfulness to their parents. If you have group members who honestly can't identify any positive part of their relationship with their parents, you may want to take time to support them in the areas they have expressed personal struggle or need.

PUTTING YOURSELF IN THE PICTURE

Let the group members know you will be providing time at the beginning of the next meeting for them to discuss how they have put their faith into action. Let them tell about how they have acted on one of the two options above. However, don't limit their interaction to these two options. They may have put themselves into the picture in some other way as a result of your study. Allow for honest and open communication.

Also, be clear that there will not be any kind of a "test" or forced reporting. All you are going to do is allow time for people to volunteer to talk about how they have applied what they learned in your last study. Some group members will feel pressured if they think you are going to make everyone report on how they acted on these action goals. You don't want anyone to skip the next meeting because they are afraid of having to say they did not follow up on what they learned from the prior session. The key is to provide a place for honest communication without creating pressure and fear of being embarrassed.

Every session from this point on will open with a look back at the "Putting Yourself in the Picture" section of the previous session.

HOW ARE YOU WIRED?

2 CORINTHIANS 6:14—18

INTRODUCTION

This session focuses on how God has designed each of us. So often husbands and wives come at life from dramatically different perspectives. The way we look at things and respond to situations can create tension in our marriage when we both have different response patterns and ways of looking at life. In this session we will honestly reflect on some of the core parts of our personalities.

Our goal is not to define who is wrong and who is right. As a matter of fact, the various kinds of behavior patterns discussed in this session are all equally valuable. Our goal is to understand our own patterns and those of our spouse so that we can more effectively understand, love, and communicate with our spouse.

THE BIG PICTURE

Take time to read this introduction with the group. There are some suggestions for how this can be done in the beginning of the leader's section.

A WIDE ANGLE VIEW

Question Two Lynne's and my failure to pay careful attention to our personality differences was a mistake for which we have paid a high price. We are convinced that the history of our marriage could have been written in far more pleasant terms if we had stumbled upon the ideas presented in this study during our courtship rather than fourteen years into our marriage.

Some of the ideas presented in the next few pages were previously discussed in *Honest to God?* (a book I wrote about being authentic), in a chapter called "Mutually Satisfying Marriage." I think they are so important, however, that I decided to present them in an updated form in this study.

Experts in the field of personality development teach that just as human beings are born with blue eyes or brown eyes, with black hair or blond hair, tall or short, so they are born with predispositions toward certain ways of thinking, behaving, and viewing the world. In the 1950s Isabel Myers and Katharine Briggs expanded on Carl Jung's work on differing temperament traits and devised a test for identifying personality types based on varying combinations of these inborn traits. This test became known as the Myers-Briggs Type Indicator.

One book that takes an in-depth look at Jung's theory and the applications made by Myers and Briggs is *Please Understand Me* by David Keirsey and Marilyn Bates. It has been of great help to me. By focusing on four aspects of thought and behavior, this book has helped me see some of the different ways in which people approach thinking and behaving. These diverse ways of thinking or behaving are called preferences. Each preference spans a continuum from mild to moderate to extreme. If you find it easy to "see yourself" in a given description in this study, you probably have an extreme preference in that area. If the picture isn't quite as clear, you may have only a mild preference.

A BIBLICAL PORTRAIT

Read 2 Corinthians 6:14–18

Question Three The process of yoking in New Testament times was understood by almost everyone: Two animals, often oxen, were yoked (connected) together for the purpose of pulling a plow or a large load. If the animals were not of equal size and strength, both could end up being injured because they did not walk with a similar stride or pull with equal strength.

The apostle Paul used this image as he warned followers of Christ not to be bound together with nonbelievers. On this earth, there is no closer yoking or connection with another human being than marriage. If a fully devoted follower of Christ marries a non-Christian, there is no way they can walk in stride together. A Christian has a whole different set of values and goals for life. If Christ is first in our lives, the idea of deciding to unite in a lifetime covenant with someone who does not know Jesus is not even an option.

SHARPENING THE FOCUS

Read Snapshot "Introverts and Extroverts" before Question 4

Question Four The first potential difference deals with sources of emotional energy and how they affect people's relational patterns. Some people are *introverts* who derive energy from solitude. They enjoy spending lots of time alone and usually tend toward pursuits that afford quiet isolation. An extreme introvert might choose to go jogging alone rather than join an exercise class and would be more likely to read a self-help book than attend a personal growth seminar. If you ever see anyone playing eighteen holes of golf alone, you can bet he or she is an introvert.

Extroverts derive emotional energy from interaction with others. They love talking, communicating, and mixing with others as much as possible. Rather than enjoying a quiet night at home, they often ask, "Who can we call to invite over?" or "Who can we go out with?" This is just how they are wired. They love to be with others.

It is critical to emphasize that neither of these personality traits are bad or wrong. They are both healthy and can reflect just how God has made a person. The focus of this study is to help couples identify how they are wired and how their spouse is wired. Understanding this will help them both learn to interact more carefully and meaningfully with each other.

Read Snapshot "Sensers and Intuitives" before Question 5

Question Five Sensers are unusually accurate in observing detail because they prefer to take in information through their senses: what they see, hear, smell, feel, and touch. After parties sensers can often describe in accurate detail what all the guests wore, exactly how the room was decorated, and what songs played in the background. If asked to describe the event, extreme sensers would likely provide more details than many of their listeners would care to know.

After parties, intuitives may well remember only those details related to their current preoccupation. If asked to describe the evening, extreme intuitives would likely sum it up in a metaphor, and leave their sensing listeners feeling "in the dark" and longing for more concrete information.

While sensers solve problems through careful analysis of the facts, intuitives often find complex solutions coming to them "out of nowhere." These frequent hunches lead intuitives down a variety of paths; in fact, they tend to skip from one activity to the next, often relying on others to finish what they started. They are often "big-picture" people who need someone else—usually a senser—to fill in the details. Sensers often see intuitives as flighty, impractical, and unrealistic, while intuitives accuse sensers of being mired in minutiae and slow to see possibilities.

Read Snapshot "Thinkers and Feelers" before Question 6

Question Six A manager who is a thinker says, with little trauma or emotion, "I'm sorry, Joe. We've adjusted your job description three times, and you're still not making the grade. It will be better for the company and for you if you look for something else." A teacher who is a thinker says, "You should have stayed after school if you didn't understand the assignment. I can't change your grade now. That would be unfair to the kids who did the assignment properly." A parent who is a thinker says, "Don't argue with me, Tony. You knew the rules and you broke them. Now you have to pay the consequences. I hope you learn your lesson."

Feelers in management agonize over difficult personnel decisions. "Yes, you're right. Joe probably will be better off in another job. But he has tried so hard, and I hate to make him feel like a failure." Feelers in education lose sleep over children who don't make the grade. "I know Angela really doesn't deserve a better grade. But I hate to penalize her for misunderstanding the assignment." Feelers who are parents really mean it when they say to their kids, "This hurts me more than it hurts you."

Thinking and feeling preferences have nothing to do with levels of intelligence or the ability to analyze and get to the root of complex issues. The question is: Once I see the issue, is it more natural for me to decide according to my head or according my heart?

Read Snapshot "Initiators and Responders" before Question 7

Question Seven The difference between initiators and responders is evident in a variety of situations. We have observed on our son's sports teams that children who are initiators tend to excel at offense, while responders often excel at defense. Young responders frequently seem to feel more comfortable defending their nets against oncoming soccer balls than trying to create action on the front line. Meanwhile, initiators seem to prefer the challenge of scoring goals.

This list is far from exhaustive. There is an almost infinite number of ways in which people can and do differ. And that is great. The intermingling of diverse personalities, unique outlooks, and complementary strengths is often the key to success in the marketplace, in education, in the church, in family life, and even in marriage.

The old adage about opposites attracting tends to be true, and for good reason. Opposites challenge one another, enhance one another, and, especially during courtship, fascinate one another. But the fascination often leads to frustration. Though we are drawn to people who are different from us, we have a hard time figuring them out. Eventually the mystery leads to misunderstanding, and too often the misunderstanding leads to maligning. It can get downright ugly.

A previously adoring couple ends up trading blatant put-downs: *You don't make sense. You are strange. There is something wrong with you. Why aren't you normal like me?* The ultimate odd couple, they come to the only conclusion that seems to make sense: they married the wrong person.

But did they? Would they really be better off if they had married someone just like them?

PUTTING YOURSELF IN THE PICTURE

Challenge group members to take time in the coming week and use part or all of this application section as an opportunity for continued growth.

Planning for Peace

Ephesians 4:25—26

Introduction

Conflict in relationships is inevitable. This is true of all relationships, but particularly of marriages. When two people from different families and backgrounds seek to join together and form a new family, there will always be tensions and potential problems. The question is not if there will be struggles and conflict in a marriage. The real issue is, when they come, how will we respond and deal with them?

It is inexcusable that couples are allowed to marry without taking mandatory conflict resolution lessons. Yet it happens all the time. Teachers, pastors, parents, and friends sit idly by and watch starry-eyed lovers overdose on romance and infatuation, knowing full well that eventually reality will strike with a vengeance, conflicts will arise, hostilities will brew, and the once blissful couple will face an emergency that neither partner will be prepared to face. Because they have not been coached or trained, they will have no emergency procedures to fall back on.

So what will they do? In most cases, they will resort to the only conflict resolution procedures they are familiar with: the ones their parents used. Even if they witnessed an unhealthy, unacceptable method of conflict resolution, and even if they vowed they would never behave that way, in the absence of proper training, they will almost inevitably revert to the method with which they grew up.

The focus of this study is to help couples identify negative patterns and resist them, as well as to develop new and healthy patterns as to how they deal with conflict in their marriage relationship.

The Big Picture

Take time to read this introduction with the group. There are some suggestions for how this can be done in the beginning of the leader's section.

A Wide Angle View

Question One These questions are not meant to lead the group members to define just the right response. They are meant to identify an honest and realistic look at conflict in human relationships. Allow your group members to give their counsel and listen closely. You will learn a great deal about the patterns and perspectives among people in your group.

A Biblical Portrait

Read Ephesians 4:25–26

Question Three The apostle Paul addresses at least two different concerns in this passage. First, he calls us to speak the truth. As always, this should be done in love, but it must be done. To swallow our own feelings and try to keep them inside is to invite disaster. This can lead to emotional distancing, resentment, and even physical and psychological sickness. Swallowing our feelings and bottling everything up inside will never lead to healing or authentic love in a marriage relationship.

Paul is also clear about the need to deal with our anger. We should not let it go unattended for too long. We read a serious warning about the devil getting a foothold when anger rules in our heart. When we live with unresolved anger, our marriage can be filled with resentment, communication may break down, love becomes hard to find, and some marriages end up shipwrecked. This breaks the heart of God. He desires healthy and loving relationships and the devil loves to tear Christian couples apart. We need to take this warning seriously and deal with our anger appropriately.

Sharpening the Focus

Read Snapshot "What We Learned" before Question 4

Question Four This will be a very tender topic of discussion for some in your group. There may be painful memories and even practices in their own relationship they are fearful to discuss. Allow people to talk as they feel able.

Here is a little more detail on the various styles of dealing with conflict:

Freeze 'Em Out. Some people fall back on the arctic style of handling conflict. In a home where this method is used, everyone knows there is a conflict; they can feel it in the air. But nobody talks about it. No matter how large the problem looms, it is never dealt with openly. People negotiate around it, avoid it, or hope that time will thaw things out. And sometimes the climate does warm up enough for people to start talking again. But the nice weather lasts only until the next conflict, which will probably focus on the same unresolved issue that caused conflict before. In a family like this, nothing is ever really worked through.

In other arctic homes the chill never leaves the air. With each new conflict, family members add another layer of ice. Eventually they freeze themselves into total withdrawal from one another.

Let the Bullets Fly. Some families handle conflict cowboy-style. When a problem surfaces or a misunderstanding arises, they square off and start shooting verbal bullets. "This town ain't big enough for the two of us," they announce. Then they shout and throw things and break windows in the saloon. Intimidation is the name of the game. Feelings are vented. Anger is released. There is action and drama. But a lot of damage is done along the way. Feelings are hurt, and children hear things they should never have to hear. And the issues that drove people apart remain unresolved.

Let Me Out of Here. Some people deal with conflict by escaping. A family conflict arises, so someone goes out and gets drunk. Another escapist might go on a shopping spree. Somebody else takes drugs. Or walks out for two or three days. Another out is workaholism. The trauma of the self-destructive escapes or the thoughtless disappearing acts tends to cloud the original issue. Issues are not faced, and problems are not solved. There is relief when the husband quits drinking or when the wife finally comes home. The problem hasn't been solved, but at least the escapist is home and under control. Until the next conflict.

I Don't Know What Happened. Sadly, some people react to conflict by manhandling others. They allow verbal assault to escalate into physical violence, and they create more pain and distance than the original issue could possibly have caused. Young people who grew up in violent homes usually vow to break that pattern of pain. But too often violence breeds violence. In spite of their good intentions, they resort to what they know.

Read Snapshot "The Spirit of Reconciliation" before Question 5

Question Five We need to acknowledge that we have fallen short of the moral standards of our holy God and that we are therefore in conflict with Him. Some of us do a pretty good job of not thinking about this, but most of us, during our semi-annual moments of introspection, get a little nervous about someday standing before a holy God. We feel a bit uneasy. We sense a latent fear of reprisal or punishment. And we know we can't do anything to escape it. Our past sins won't disappear, and God's holiness won't change. So we are stuck in an unresolvable and unwinnable conflict.

Coming to grips with our desperate position is the first step toward a spirit of reconciliation. The second step is to realize that God, "being rich in mercy," offered His Son, Jesus Christ, to bridge the chasm of conflict that separates us from God. Through Jesus' death and resurrection, we can be reconciled to God and freed from the fear of condemnation and eternal death. We can be adopted into God's family and relate to Him as a much-loved child relates to a kind father.

The third step toward a reconciling spirit happens naturally to those who have been adopted into God's family and are growing spiritually. The joy of divine reconciliation begins to spill over into other areas of their lives. They want to experience the peace and harmony they enjoy with God and with others. They begin to understand that all people—friends, family members, strangers, even enemies—matter to God. The chunks of ice in their chests begin to melt, and they feel concern and compassion for people they previously ignored or spurned or mistreated.

The Bible tells of a wealthy tax collector who routinely ripped people off without the slightest appearance of remorse—until he had a heart-to-heart with Jesus Christ over an unscheduled dinner. After a simple meal and a brief conversation, this hard-hearted extortionist emerged from his house a transformed man. With trembling lips he begged the forgiveness of those he had cheated and promised to repay them four times over. He even vowed to give half of all his future earnings to the poor.

Something supernatural happened at that dinner table. Not only was a sinner reconciled to God, but he also received the spirit of reconciliation, which turned his feelings toward people upside down. And what happened to Zacchaeus is the norm for all who become reconciled to God. The Holy Spirit plants within them an appreciation for others that wasn't there before. He gives them a longer fuse, more patience, an increased capacity to forgive, a heightened desire for harmony, a sensitivity and tenderness that they never felt before.

**Read Snapshot "Is That a Plank in Your Eye?"
before Question 6**

Question Six Explain that you will be doing two different
things at this time. First, you will be allowing a few minutes
for personal prayer and reflection. Allow time for God to show
group members where they may have a "plank" in their eye.
Encourage them to be open to any conviction of the Holy
Spirit about how they might be bringing tension, pain, or hurt
to their spouse. You may even want to open this time with a
prayer for each person to be sensitive and open to what God
wants to put on their heart.

Next, break the group into couples. Encourage them to spend
a few minutes telling each other where they feel they need to
improve in their relationship. Encourage them to confess to
each other where they see a "plank" in their own eye and to
discuss how they can work on this area of their relationship.

For many people the normal reaction to relational hurt,
misunderstanding, or attack is to strike back. To get even. To
fix blame. To say, "It's your fault." We have all behaved that
way on occasion. What's more, we have probably felt justi-
fied. *What's right is right*, we say. *If you get hurt, you gotta get even.
I shouldn't have to put up with this. Retaliation is self-preservation.*
Then we self-righteously spin on our heel, and walk out
(slamming the door behind us), straight to the relational
graveyard. We can't stand the discomfort and turmoil of relational tension, and we see no way to fix it. So we get out the
shovel, bury the relationship, and try to get on with life. But
we live with a dull, aching pain that won't go away.

This will be an opportunity to seek to reverse this damaging
process and seek honest communication and reconciliation.
This process will begin with humble prayer, listening to God,
and honest confession of where we have fallen short in our
responsibility as a husband or wife.

Read Snapshot "Can We Talk?" before Question 7

Question Seven A broadened description of the guidelines
for conflict resolution follows.

Begin with affirmation. Learning to begin with affirmation helped
Lynne and me start our discussions from a positive position.
We used to jump right into the problem, which meant we
were starting the discussion from a negative position. Doing
that almost always polarized us and elicited defensive
responses.

Beginning with affirmation softened the blow of the conflict and kept us from reeling into defensiveness. Our peace talks became much more peaceful when we learned to say, "Honey, I love you and I am committed to our marriage. But I think it can be better than it is. Here are some ideas I have." An introduction like that can lead to a constructive conversation.

Be willing to take blame. Bring to the meeting the insights and attitudes that were fostered during your time of private prayer. Acknowledge specifically how you contributed to the tension. Do not take blame you don't deserve, but fully accept what is rightly yours.

"I'm sorry I was so selfish."

"Forgive me for letting my ego get in the way."

"I feel horrible about blowing up in front of the kids."

You will be amazed at the power of apology. Two short words— I'm sorry—have saved business partnerships, reconciled neighbors, reunited fathers and sons, and rescued marriages that were headed for the graveyard. There is no magic in the words themselves, but when they are said sincerely they reveal what is underneath—the spirit of reconciliation. And they open up the lines of communication.

When Zacchaeus, the reformed tax collector, ran out into the streets, the people who knew him probably ran in the opposite direction. "How is he going to cheat us this time?" they wondered. "What new scam has he concocted?" But apparently he stopped them dead in their tracks. How? He said, "I'm sorry. I was wrong. I cheated you. I want to make it right." They were probably suspicious; they probably had a wait-and-see attitude. But like most people, they wanted to believe the best. So they listened. They opened their hearts. And Zacchaeus's apology opened the way for healing and restitution.

Express hurt instead of hostility. Most problems start with hurt. A wife feels hurt because her husband didn't ask about a presentation she made at work that day. Or because he forgot their anniversary. Or was unnecessarily critical of her mother. A husband feels hurt because his wife didn't notice the weight he lost. Or because she wasn't sensitive about a pressure at work. Or she insulted him in front of a friend.

Hurt is a legitimate response to disappointment and offense, and it should never be denied or kept hidden inside. It should always be expressed and discussed. But hurt becomes a problem when people let it build up inside and turn into anger. The wife starts out being hurt by her husband's apparent lack of interest in her career, but after she mulls the hurt around in her mind for a while, it becomes infected. She ends up being angry at "the insensitive louse who only cares about what he does."

This is why it is important to plan peace talks as soon as possible, before hurt turns to anger. Most people are moved by another person's pain, so revealing hurt can build bridges of understanding and compassion. But venting hostility blows up bridges, because people are repelled by angry assaults. When someone attacks, our natural reaction is to fight back.

Another mistake that causes hurt to turn to anger is accumulating grievances. One hurt is manageable. You can keep it under control, express it constructively, and work through it. Two hurts are a little harder to deal with. Accumulate more than that and it is almost impossible to keep them from comparing notes and deciding that they deserve to turn into anger.

So please deal with grievances as they arise. Don't stack them on top of one another or let them fester inside until they turn to hostility. Anger is always a secondary emotion. If spouses back up to what preceded it, they will often find hurt. If they reveal the hurt, they will weaken the walls that separate them.

Make direct statements. Hints and offhand remarks accomplish little. Whether we are in the midst of a formal peace talk or a casual conversation, we must say what we mean.

Make "I Feel" statements. Many peace plans are sabotaged by "you" statements of accusation that antagonize spouses and often terminate the peace process before it even starts.

- "You don't help enough around the house."
- "You spend too much time at work."
- "You don't know how to handle money."

"I feel" statements are much less inflammatory and open the door for further discussion and practical problem solving.

- "I feel overwhelmed by household responsibilities. I have thought of some ways we might be able to divide up the tasks. Can I tell you about them?"
- "I often feel left out of your life because you spend so much time at work. Can we talk about that?"
- "I feel frustrated about our financial situation. Would you be willing to discuss some ways to keep our budget in better order?"

Avoid "never" and "always." Avoid speaking in exaggerated terms such as

- "You never come home on time."

- "You always forget to call."
- "You are forever leaving dirty dishes in the family room."

We may have a perfectly reasonable concern, but if we express it in extreme terms, we invalidate it. We turn the truth into a lie.

If we want our grievances to be taken seriously, we must make accurate, truthful, realistic statements. *Always* and *never* will always—well, almost always—shift the focus away from the real issue. The unreasonably accused spouse will probably dismiss the original concern and blame the relational tension on the other spouse's poor communication techniques.

Question Eight What if your peace talks aren't working? What if you can't stay on track? What if you constantly go forward one inch and back two? The next step is to seek counsel from a trusted friend or couple. Proverbs 11:14 says, "For lack of guidance a nation falls, but many advisers make victory sure."

I shudder to think where Lynne and I would be without the wise, insightful, and sometimes painful counsel we have received from trusted friends. When you have close friends who will pray for you, encourage you, and keep you accountable in your marriage, you have a wonderful gift. These people love you enough to ask the hard questions and sharpen your life.

A friend once told me, "You're too frugal with your wife. You're liberal when it comes to giving to God's work. You're liberal with your kids. You're liberal when your friends are in need. But you're pretty cheap with your wife. You need to be more generous with her."

Another friend said, "You ought to take more interest in your house and yard. You enjoy having an orderly, well-maintained refuge to come home to, but you don't take enough responsibility for keeping it that way."

I didn't like hearing those things, but I needed to hear them. They were true, and they were building walls in my relationship with Lynne. I'm thankful I had friends who knew me and loved me enough to take the risk of telling me the truth. And I'm thankful that I had learned the value of accepting hard counsel.

We have also benefited from seeking counsel together from another couple. "What advice can you give us about this situation?" we ask. "How do you compromise in this area? How have you solved this problem?" At times we have had to schedule formal peace talks with our friends. Sometimes we just use casual get-togethers as opportunities to glean insight from married couples we respect.

PUTTING YOURSELF IN THE PICTURE

Challenge group members to take time in the coming week to use part or all of this application section as an opportunity for continued growth.

CALL IN THE PROFESSIONALS

Here are a few thoughts for those who are struggling and need additional support at this time in their marriage. If you sense there are some in your group who need more help than discussed in this session, you may want to suggest marriage counseling from a competent Christian counselor.

Some people refuse to seek counsel because they are embarrassed; they don't want anyone to know their marriage is a bit frayed around the edges. Some people refuse because they are afraid to face a painful truth, or afraid of what they might learn about themselves or their spouse. Others refuse because they are stubborn and cruel. They would rather dismantle the emotional health of their spouse than expend the energy to get help. Still others question the theological "rightness" of seeking professional Christ-centered counsel: "Shouldn't we be able to pray ourselves out of this problem? Shouldn't we be able to find an answer in the Bible?"

Prayer and Bible study are vital elements in marital health. However, God has gifted certain individuals with a degree of discernment, knowledge, and wisdom that allows them to assist couples who occasionally hit impasses, or couples who are stuck in unhealthy, destructive patterns of relating.

Some couples get stuck for so long they forget what a good marriage is like. They begin to settle for a mediocre marriage, or even for a miserable one. They need somebody to refresh their minds and teach them how to get back to a healthy, positive, loving way of relating.

Sometimes only one spouse is willing to seek counsel. I would encourage that partner to go alone. It is better for one partner to get unstuck than for both to remain where they are. We have seen God do amazing things through one spouse who is willing to face the challenge of growth. Many times the unwilling spouse is impacted by the visible change in the other.

Conflict resolution requires courage and persistence. It calls for humility and honesty. It chips away at our hardness of heart, and sometimes it produces pain. But it is always worth whatever effort it takes, whatever inconvenience it causes, and whatever change or compromise it requires.

WHATEVER HAPPENED TO ROMANCE?

SONG OF SONGS 4

INTRODUCTION

We all want romance in our marriage. No one sets out on the adventure of marriage and says, "You know what, three years into this thing I hope I no longer feel any romantic excitement." We all want and expect to be just as madly in love with our spouse ten years down the line as we were on our wedding day.

The problem is, so many couples find a whole different experience. As the years go on, romance seems to wane. Our intentions were good, but we often put little effort into developing an exciting and romantic marriage. The basic inertia of life drags us down, and romance is one of the first things to go.

This study will help your group members identify some of the "Romance Busters" that sap the excitement and romance out of marriage. It will also help couples identify ways they can remove some of these barriers and move toward a more romantic and fulfilling marriage.

THE BIG PICTURE

Take time to read this introduction with the group. There are some suggestions for how this can be done in the beginning of the leader's section.

A WIDE ANGLE VIEW

Question One Lynne and I are no exception when it comes to struggling with keeping the romance alive in our marriage. Lynne recounts an experience she had several years into our marriage.

> Over lunch in a local restaurant, Bill and I listened while a middle-aged consultant for an international manufacturing firm lamented having to spend so much time away from his wife.

"I make the best of it though," he said. "I call her every night and we talk about what happened during the day. I send her lots of little notes and cards just to remind her I'm thinking about her. If I travel to interesting places I buy her jewelry that is representative of the area. And I always come home with lingerie—something fun and flirtatious that puts us in the mood for romance. We have to be apart so often, we want to make the time we have together count!"

He mentioned his wife several other times during the conversation, and it became obvious that after twenty-five years of marriage he was still "crazy in love" with her. He still treasured her. He still looked forward to being with her. He still had fun with her. He still got a kick out of making love to her.

As I listened, I found myself being strangely attracted to this man, and it frightened me. I didn't understand it. There I was, sitting next to my handsome, successful young husband to whom I was wholeheartedly committed. Yet I was feeling drawn to a fiftyish grandfather who talked nonstop about his wife. What was going on?

Throughout the afternoon I pondered the conversation and finally realized that the reason I felt drawn to that man was that I longed to be loved and treasured the way he loved and treasured his wife. I wanted to feel special, to be pursued, to know that my husband delighted in me—and that wasn't happening in our marriage at that point.

I had to say, "I love you, Bill, and I am more committed to our marriage than I have ever been. But we've lost something along the way. Our marriage seems more like a business, a partnership, a joint venture, than like an intimate, loving union. We struggle along, trying to live in peace as best we can, but there is too little spark in our relationship. Too little fun. Too little romance. I don't want to go on like this anymore. Marriage should be so much more than this. We should be so much happier than we are. We need to get the romance back."

A Biblical Portrait

Read Song of Songs 4

Question Three Song of Songs is a praise of romantic love between a man and a woman. We must understand that God's plan from the very beginning of time was for a man and a woman to share their lives together in the most intimate relationship.

Romantic love was and still is God's design. He rejoices when husbands and wives are so committed to their spouse that they will work at nurturing and building a healthy and romantic relationship. God's desire is for followers of Christ to model

marriage relationships full of emotional intimacy, open communication, sexual passion, and spiritual wholeness. It is
important for us to remember that God's plan of a man and a
woman in intimate relationship was instituted before sin
entered the world.

SHARPENING THE FOCUS

Read Snapshot "Romance Busters" before Question 4

Question Five A number of factors drain the romance out of
marriage. One is *the curse of familiarity*. It happens in all arenas
of life. You buy a new car and for a few weeks you create
reasons to go to the store so you can drive it. You wash it on
lunch break. You make your kids shower before they get near
it. But after a while, without even realizing it, you begin treat-
ing your new car the way you treated the old one. You let the
dog crawl around in it. You let the kids drink milk shakes in it.
You say, "I don't have to worship this. It's just a car."

The same thing happens when you buy a new house, a new
piece of furniture, or a new item of clothing. For a while you
treat it so carefully, but once the shine wears off and the glitter
fades—once familiarity sets in—you quit protecting it and
worrying about it and caring for it so meticulously.

Unfortunately, we often treat people the same way we treat
purchases. During the courtship phase, when a guy arrives to
pick up his girlfriend for a date, he barely touches the doorbell
before the door swings wide open and she says, "Oh, Tom,
I've been thinking about you all day. I've been counting the
ticks of the clock. I thought you would never arrive." After
two years of marriage, Tom comes home from work forty-
five minutes late and announces, "I'm home, honey." His wife
says, "So am I. What do you want, a marching band?"

A twisted sense of security can also drain the romance out of
marriage. During the courtship phase, partners live with the
nagging fear that if they don't stay on their toes, if they aren't
thoughtful and courteous, if they don't communicate creatively,
if they don't "beat the competition," they might lose the relationship. Once they are married, however, some people get a
little too complacent. They feel a little too secure. They get
careless, thoughtless, and matter-of-fact about their relationship.

Physical exhaustion can also drain the romance out of marriage.
When do most people have their highest levels of energy?
During their late teens and early twenties—when they are
courting. With time and boundless energy their romance

flourishes. They go out on dates five nights a week. Stay up talking till 2 A.M. Schedule breakfast meetings before dawn so they can watch the sunrise. Many college couples do what we did. As soon as the young man's Friday afternoon class ends, he jumps in his car and drives several hours to his girlfriend's college, where he spends a day and a half with her before driving back to his campus for his Monday morning class. The next weekend she visits him.

But few couples can maintain that pace over the long haul. During the coming years their energy levels seem to plummet. What really complicates things is that at the same time their energy drops, their *responsibilities skyrocket.* Career. Kids. Car pools. The PTA. The handyman special they call a house. In-law challenges. Church involvement. Community service. And then they look in the mirror and notice that their bodies need a little attention, so they try to squeeze in some exercise.

In addition to increased responsibility and time commitments, there is often an *increased financial burden.* During courtship many young people live with parents or roommates and have minimal living expenses. So they have plenty of excess money to spend on dates. One young man told us about renting a tux to wear to take his girlfriend out for dinner—just for fun. We thought, *Wait till that guy gets married. Wait till he's making house payments and buying cars and furniture. And wait till he's raising kids.* Kids are fun, but they are costly little critters. Who thinks about long-stemmed roses and romantic dinners when you need a crib, a lawn mower, and a new roof?

As the years pass, life gets more and more complicated. What usually takes the brunt of all the madness? Marriage. *He can wait. She will understand. We'll attend to the marriage later, when we have more time, more energy, more creativity, and more money.*

But we know that seldom happens.

Read Snapshot "Shifting Gears" before Question 6

Question Six Provide time for personal reflection and prayer. Encourage group members to be honest with themselves and God as they ask themselves the questions.

In the snapshot I talked about the damaging process of shifting gears after the wedding day. Here is a more detailed description of how this process can happen in some marriages:

> The journey begins like this. A young man identifies the woman he wants to marry and begins the business of serious courtship. Time and money are no object, so he throws vast amounts of energy and creativity into the pursuit. He gives

gifts, sends cards, writes poems, delivers flowers, plans romantic dinners in elegant restaurants, takes long walks on sandy beaches, enjoys leisurely drives on country roads, and loiters in front of glittering jewelry store windows. He is on a mission. He has a worthy goal. He is motivated. He lets nothing stand in the way of winning the woman of his dreams. She becomes his top priority, and he will not rest until she is his.

He is smitten and he wants her to know it. He rearranges his busy schedule to spend every possible minute with her. He compliments her warmly. He sings her praises to friends and family. He talks about her constantly. And very slowly he begins to wear her down.

That's right, wear her down. You see, she was a little suspicious at first. He was obviously in hot pursuit, but what exactly did that mean? What was he after? Did he want a cheap thrill or a lasting relationship? A female trophy or a wife he could treasure? She knows the dangers because she has been hurt before. So she wisely guards her heart and maintains her distance. She observes, waits, and analyzes. Can this guy be trusted? Or will he dash her dreams six months after the wedding? She has heard the horror stories, and doesn't intend to provide the plot for another one.

Meanwhile, the diligent young man showers her with attention, affection, and appreciation. He calls her four times a day, fills her mailbox with declarations of love, and buys her sentimental gifts and exotic perfumes. The weekends are wall-to-wall recreation and romance: dinners, movies, plays, parties. And now—the offer of a diamond ring.

Almost against her will, she feels loved. She feels safe and secure and treasured and prized and wanted. She begins to trust him. She begins to believe that it will last. In fact, she lets herself believe that it will keep getting better and better and that marriage will open the door to a future of unimagined joy.

Finally, the last bridge of doubt is crossed and she says, "Yes, yes, I will marry you. You have proven beyond a shadow of doubt that you love me. You have courted me, romanced me, made me feel special and important and treasured. You have convinced me that I am at the top of your priority list. You have won my heart. I will marry you!"

So the wedding date is set, the ceremony is carefully planned, and the honeymoon is arranged. It all comes off in storybook style. The newly married couple move into their cozy studio apartment and the young wife settles into the realities of everyday married life, reveling in the knowledge that she made a wise and wonderful choice for a lifetime partner.

And then it happens. Her husband does a terrible, horrible, awful, unthinkable, rotten, reprehensible thing. Oh, he doesn't realize he is doing anything wrong. But he does it, nonetheless, and deeply wounds his sincere, trusting wife.

What does he do? He shifts gears. He readjusts his focus. He figures that now that he got the "marriage job" done, it is time to move on to another objective. He faced one challenge and beat it; now it is time to face another one. So without giving one thought to how this is going to affect his wife, he calmly rearranges his priorities, reapportions his energies, and launches out on his next mission, most likely in the marketplace.

There is no malice in his decision. In fact, he is probably not even aware that he is making the shift. If questioned about his love for his wife, he would deny that it has faltered in the least. He loves her as much as he did the day he married her. He is simply doing what he has been conditioned to do.

Most men don't intend to hurt their wives. They do what they do without thinking. And, as we mentioned earlier, husbands aren't the only ones who fall into this pattern. The unprecedented entrance of women into the marketplace has put wives at equal risk when it comes to refocusing their energies and neglecting romance. In many marriages nowadays, both spouses make the destructive shift. A young couple we know were best friends all through high school, dated happily throughout college, and married with the total blessing of family and friends. But five years into marriage they sat across from one another on their living room floor, weeping over the lack of feeling in their marriage. They weren't spiritually incompatible. They hadn't lost respect for one another. They didn't have serious temperament clashes or poor conflict resolution skills. They had simply poured themselves into their careers and neglected to treasure one another.

We recently attended a small conference with a number of couples in the fifty- to sixty-year age range. We observed that many of the men were unusually attentive toward their wives. Because we were in the midst of working on this book, we asked them why. Almost without exception, the men said, "This is my second wife. During my first marriage I was too preoccupied with climbing the corporate ladder to pay attention to my wife. I hurt her deeply for many years, and finally she couldn't take it anymore. Now I'm doing things differently. I may have forfeited my first wife, but I'm not going to foul things up again."

While some people let their careers get in the way of romance, others get sidetracked by parenting. They get so caught up in child-rearing responsibilities that they forget they are husbands and wives first, parents second. In attempting to give their best to their children, they fail to give them what they need most: a happily married mom and dad.

Question Seven Provide time for couples to talk together and reflect on the questions. If possible, allow them to move to places where they can talk privately. Have the group gather together for a closing time of encouragement and accountability.

PUTTING YOURSELF IN THE PICTURE

Challenge group members to take time in the coming week to use part or all of this application section as an opportunity for continued growth.

FANNING THE FLAMES OF MARRIAGE

1 CORINTHIANS 7:3—5

INTRODUCTION

Can a battered romance be rebuilt? Can the smoldering embers of dying feelings be refueled? I think they can be. I think that the love that drew a couple together in courtship can be recaptured and sustained in spite of disappointments and setbacks and stormy weather. In this session I want to give some practical suggestions for doing just that.

The road back may not be easy. The flames may have burned down, but there are ways to fan them back into a fire. This is God's desire for every couple.

THE BIG PICTURE

Take time to read this introduction with the group. There are some suggestions for how this can be done in the beginning of the leader's section.

A WIDE ANGLE VIEW

Question One Allow time for couples to reminisce on some of the good times they have experienced over the years of their relationship. Also, encourage honest discussion of some of the tough times and struggles they have faced.

A BIBLICAL PORTRAIT

Read 1 Corinthians 7:3–5

Question Three Paul is clear that prolonged abstinence in marriage is not healthy. Each spouse must realize that they do not only belong to themselves but also to their marriage partner. Healthy and regular sexual expression should be a part of every Christian marriage.

When a couple goes for prolonged periods of time without sexual expression, there is potential for temptation. Paul clearly warns us that the enemy will use this as an opportunity to appeal to a man's or a woman's lack of self-control.

This in no way gives a person an excuse for unfaithfulness or inappropriate sexual behavior. It is simply a clear warning that couples who don't take seriously the need for a healthy sexual relationship are inviting problems and temptations.

If we are going to fan the flames of romance and marriage, there needs to be a commitment to grow in the area of sexual expression as well as other areas of intimacy.

This topic will be discussed later in this session.

Sharpening the Focus

Read Snapshot "Talk, Talk, Talk" before Question 4

Question Four Some years ago our teenage daughter was dating a young man with whom she spent a Saturday afternoon. They ran a few errands, then sat on a picnic table in a forest preserve and talked. "You talked?" we asked. "All afternoon? About what?"

"You know. About everything. About school and church and our friends. About what we like and don't like. About what we're going to do this summer. About our goals. About college. About what makes us mad or happy. About you guys! It was wonderful."

Do you remember when there weren't enough hours in the day for you and your spouse to contain your conversations? Do you remember how close you felt? How tuned in you were to each other?

Husbands and wives ought to find comfort in one another's presence. Their marriage should be a place of refuge. There ought to be an underlying sense that "it's you and me against the world." But it will never be that way unless spouses make time for in-depth communication on a regular basis. That is why a weekly date outside the home is so important. And why we need to take advantage of every opportunity to "catch up" on what is going on with our spouses. An after-dinner conversation while the kids clear the table, or an evening walk around the block, or even an afternoon telephone call to find out what the doctor said or how things went at the meeting can keep spouses informed and build on the sense of unity and caring established during more lengthy and significant conversations.

Read Snapshot "Don't Bury the Hurt" before Question 5

Question Five Some couples can deal with past hurt through honest conversation, humble admission of their own guilt, and a commitment to change their behaviors toward their spouse. When this happens, joy can return to a marriage and romance can return.

What complicates the process is that usually both spouses have caused hurt and received it. Sometimes a counselor can help sort through the confusion and assist spouses in asserting their own pain, while at the same time being sensitive to the other's pain. Again, it is tempting to jump over this step. But taking a responsible approach to past hurts, even if that means devoting six months or a year to Christian counseling, will make the difference between smoldering embers and a roaring bonfire.

After you face up to past hurts and work through them, you can protect your new sense of unity and warmth by dealing with new conflicts as they arise. Planning frequent peace talks will clear the air and keep hurts from going underground again. Nothing destroys romance like an edge of anger. As the old adage says, it's no fun to hug a porcupine.

Read Snapshot "Court Creatively" before Question 6

Question Six Maybe you might want to start by taking a few minutes over lunch and write a simple note to your spouse. "I was just thinking about you and wanted to tell you I love you." "If I had it to do over again, I'd marry you in a minute." "I'm excited about what the future will bring." Then put it in the mail. Imagine how your spouse will feel when they read that love note.

Or you might consider calling your spouse during the day for no reason. "Hi. How are you? I was just wondering how your day was going." It means so much to a husband or wife to know that their spouse was thinking about them—and took the time to say it.

Nonsexual touching is another important part of courting. If your first response to that sentence is that it is nonsense, it is no wonder the romance has drained out of your marriage. As important as sexual touch is—and we will talk about it later— warm, loving, nonsexual touch is every bit as essential to a romance-filled marriage.

Too many spouses do little more than give each other an obligatory kiss when they part ways in the morning and then repeat the routine when they greet one another at night. Their lips touch, but they barely even know it. It has become an involuntary response. Adding a little variety to touching can take it out of the autopilot realm and put the feeling back in it. When you take an after-dinner walk, reach down and grab your spouse's hand—and think about what you are doing. Let your clasped hands symbolize the lifetime commitment you have made to one another. While your spouse reads the paper, bend down and gently rub his or her neck; think of it as a comforting act of tenderness, as a way to ease the stress of a busy day. Touch that is backed by feeling is a match that can reignite a dying flame.

Flowers still spell romance. But don't just buy the daily special. Think back to your dating days. Did your spouse have a favorite flower? Was there a special occasion marked by a red rose? Do you recall a romantic evening complete with a beautiful corsage? Get creative. On your way to dinner, present your wife with a purple orchid like the one she wore to the prom. Buy a bouquet of sweetheart roses in honor of the flowers she carried on your wedding day.

If flowers never earned a place in your memory bank, don't despair. Ask your wife what kind she likes. Chances are she won't remember—it's been so long since it mattered—but give her time. Once the shock wears off and her senses return, she will describe the perfect bouquet. Ordering precisely what she describes will tell her that her preferences, her desires, her tastes matter to you. It will say, "I still treasure you."

Dating is another important part of marriage. We have friends who always discuss their Friday night date during dinner on the previous Monday. They look through the entertainment section of the Sunday newspaper, consider various options, then decide together what they want to do. Then they have all week to anticipate their plans and remind each other in notes or calls that "We're going to have a great time on Friday night," or "It's been a long week, but we'll be able to celebrate soon." They each make the evening more special by wearing clothes the other particularly likes.

Another aspect of courting creatively is serving one another. During high school, a young man carries his girlfriend's books and she makes him chocolate chip cookies. In college he hauls her suitcases and she types his term paper. During engagement he fixes her car and she does his laundry (or vice versa).

But six months after the wedding, they retire their servant's uniforms. Suddenly it's every man for himself, every woman for herself. They hide the uniforms in the back of the hallway closet, and with them the warm feelings that service engenders. If a husband and wife want to heat up those feelings again, they need to squeeze themselves back into those uniforms, blow the dust off the shoulders, and get back to serving. Discovering and joyfully offering small acts of service that bring special delight to a spouse is a great way to change the tone of a relationship.

Creative courting also includes inspiring our spouses. Do you remember how often you used to cheer each other on when you were dating? "You have so much potential!" "You can succeed at whatever you choose." "You belong on the stage; you played that role perfectly." "I'll stand by you no matter what." "I can't wait to see you soar." "That was great how you caught that line drive this afternoon." "You have tremendous gifts and abilities." "I'm so proud of you." But now that you've settled into life's routines, do you even pay attention to what your spouse is doing? Do you comment on accomplishments or encourage after failures? Are you the biggest cheerleader your spouse has?

Read Snapshot "Language of Love" before Question 7

Question Seven Do you know which language of love is important to your spouse? For years I assumed that the best way to convince Lynne that I loved her was to remind her repeatedly why I had married her. "I really appreciate your spirituality," I'd tell her, "and your intelligence and your conscientiousness. I respect your character, and I think you'll make a great mother someday." I was sure that would make her feel loved. But it didn't. She appreciated it, but it wasn't enough to convince her of my love. She needed to receive love through the language of touch; she needed lots of physical affection. She also needed my time. She needed me to take the initiative in setting aside quiet hours on a regular basis when we could be together. For years, I gave her neither.

Why did I assume that verbal expressions of love would do the job? Because that was the love language I preferred. It made me feel great when Lynne told me she was proud of something I had done or that she loved a certain aspect of my character or personality. I didn't need her to hug me or squeeze my hand or spend large blocks of time with me, as much as I needed her to build me up with her words. I needed to know she loved and respected the unique qualities that made me *me*. So I assumed that was all she needed.

Making assumptions about the language of love our spouse prefers often leads to disappointment, and sometimes even to misunderstanding.

PUTTING YOURSELF IN THE PICTURE

Challenge group members to take time in the coming week to use part or all of this application section as an opportunity for continued growth.

ADDITIONAL LEADER'S NOTES

I encourage you to direct your group members to this section of the leader's notes for their own discussion as a couple. The topic and importance of sex cannot be ignored. However, a small group discussion might be too vulnerable for some people. For this reason I have put these notes in this portion of the study. It would be good for all of the couples in your group to read this section together.

Mutually satisfying sex starts with communication, creative courting, meaningful expressions of love, and shared fun. The actual act of sex is the culmination of a series of encounters that set the tone and create the desire for total and loving physical intimacy.

Sex should be the ultimate fun activity a couple shares. Unfortunately, for many couples, including us during the early years of our marriage, sex provides more frustration than fun. A small percentage of couples suffer from true sexual dysfunctions of either physical or psychological origins. I would encourage them to consult a doctor or a Christian counselor. Applying simplistic answers to their complex problems would only increase their frustration.

Even aside from sexual dysfunctions, human sexuality is very complex and is affected by a myriad of personal and relational factors. Obviously we cannot, in a few short pages, look in depth at such a broad subject. I have found, however, that many couples in the process of rebuilding romance can benefit from a slight shift in attitude or from a few fresh ideas regarding sexual experience. That's what Lynne and I needed.

Fun for Whom?

Like many young married couples, Lynne and I read our share of books about sex. We easily dismissed those authors who viewed sexual intercourse solely as a means of procreation, and appreciated authors who acknowledged that God has designed human sexuality, in part at least, for married people's pleasure. Such authors described sexual pleasure as a priceless gift spouses can give to one another—a gift, in fact, that they *must* give to one another.

The notion of sex as something important we must give to our spouses is biblical. First Corinthians 7 teaches clearly that spouses must fulfill their "marital duty" to one another, and must not "deprive each other." According to this passage, a wife does not have authority over her own body; her husband does. Similarly, she has authority over his. These verses are not-so-subtle reminders that we each owe our spouse a satisfying sexual relationship. We are, after all, our spouse's only sexual option. The commitment to marital fidelity, which every sincere Christian couple must make, means that if we don't find sexual fulfillment in our marriage, we don't find it. It is as simple, and sometimes as tragic, as that. Each of us must take our sexual responsibility seriously, lovingly, and enthusiastically doing everything in our power to meet and fulfill our spouse's sexual needs and desires.

Having said all that, I want to briefly mention the flip side of healthy sex. I believe that putting too much emphasis on sex as something one does for his or her spouse can have a negative effect on some people's attitudes. For these people sex becomes one more obligation, one more task they need to perform to be a "good wife" or a "good husband." They forget that sex is something they should enjoy *for themselves*.

Some people don't enjoy sex because they don't enjoy their own sexuality. Some husbands and wives, in fact, don't even view themselves as sexual beings. Sex is something they *do,* an out-of-character behavior they squeeze in at the end of a busy day, rather than a natural extension of an important dimension of who they are. These people would become more interested and interesting sexual partners if they would give themselves permission to enjoy their sexuality, view their sexuality as an important part of their identity, and take delight in excelling sexually. People who take a positive approach to their sexuality, and commit themselves to developing their sexual skills just as they develop their other gifts and skills, cultivate a sexual confidence that frees them to become active rather than passive participants in their sexual relationship. They become proactive sexually rather than merely reactive. And they bring tremendous pleasure to their spouse.

Getting Started

Fun sex doesn't start in the bedroom. It starts in the kitchen, during a private moment when a nonsexual touch slides over into the realm of the blatantly sexual. It begins with a playful suggestion of sexual intent, or a not-so-subtle sexual innuendo, or a well-placed flirtatious remark.

Over the years we have developed our own *physical love language*. When I leave for the evening and Lynne whispers, "If you make it home from your board meeting on time tonight, I'll make it worth your while," I don't have to wonder what she means. I know that's an open invitation, and you can bet I get home on time. This may explain the efficiency of our board meetings!

When I'm traveling, and I call home and Lynne says, "You don't know what you're missing tonight," I know that's her way of telling me I have an interested wife waiting at home. And it seriously tempts me to hop a plane for O'Hare.

Another way to encourage sexual enthusiasm is to actively build one another's concept of desirability. Husbands and wives will be much more interested in sex if they feel like desirable sexual partners.

How we dress is another way we can heighten—or squelch—sexual desire. Most spouses admit that what their husband or wife wears affects their sexual interest.

Maintaining good health is another way to enhance sexual interest. The general sense of well-being and increased body consciousness that come from regular exercise enhance sexuality. Eating right and getting enough sleep are important, too. Everybody knows that exhaustion is one of the greatest sex-busters.

Other sure sex-busters are hostility and lack of creativity. Working through hidden hostilities and learning to court creatively are essential to enhancing sexual interest.

Again—Talk, Talk, Talk

Each couple's physical relationship is unique. Some couples couldn't imagine a sexual encounter without music and candlelight. Others prefer silence and the cloak of darkness. For some people, exhaustion makes an evening rendezvous impractical; they prefer morning get-togethers. For others, even the thought of a morning sexual encounter is laughable. Preferred frequency of sex is also highly variable.

Instead of taking your cues from Hollywood or from other couples, why not develop your own sexual style. Experiment. Explore new avenues of sexual expression. And above all, communicate. Talk openly, vulnerably, specifically, and regularly about your sexual relationship. There is a direct correlation between a couple's level of sexual communication and their level of sexual fulfillment. Too many people expect their spouses to "just know" what they want sexually, then do a slow burn when their spouses don't figure it out.

A more constructive option is to openly discuss issues directly related to sexuality. You might suggest ways your spouse could help you feel more sexually desirable, and ask for ideas about how you could do the same in return. Another idea is to describe the kinds of circumstances, events, or conversations that are most likely to spark your sexual interest. You could also talk about guaranteed turnoffs, personal sex-busters, and past sexual disappointments. Or you could describe your best recent sexual memories, and explain what made those experiences so good. Sharing specific ideas about what you can each do, say, or wear to capture the other's sexual attention would also be helpful.

For some couples these questions are terribly threatening. Husbands and wives who have never talked openly about their sexual relationship often find it very hard to get started. Picking one question and discussing it after a day of lighthearted fun may be the best way for such couples to start. Eventually they can move into more in-depth discussions— and even begin a little undercover research!

Sensitive, open communication is a hefty challenge, whether you are discussing a backlog of anger or a way to spice up a less-than-sizzling sexual relationship. But it always pays high dividends. So give it a try. Prop up the pillows on your bed, make yourself comfortable, and talk openly with your spouse about sex. You just might be glad you did.

We were.

LIVING IN CRISIS MODE

PSALM 46

INTRODUCTION

It was just a small spot of weakness on the mythical warrior's heel, but it led to his death in the Trojan War. Since classical times, we have borrowed from the Greek legend the notion of a nagging vulnerability with the power to bring a strong man—or woman—down. Everyone has an "Achilles' heel." The wise among us, who recognize their weaknesses and carefully protect them from attack, stand firm; the unwise, who leave their weaknesses exposed, are downed in the battle.

One problem with an Achilles' heel—whatever form it takes—is that it follows us into marriage. In this study we will look at an Achilles' heel that seems to nag so many couples today. We live in a society that is driven. Many men and women live with incredible stress because of busy schedules, overcommitment, and workaholism. It's no wonder so many marriages are suffering. In many marriages, one or both of the partners are living with the RPMs of their life in the red almost all of the time.

We need to learn how to slow down. In the midst of the business of life we need to be still and know that God is in control. We also need to learn how to slow down our pace and to discover how to recharge our emotional batteries when they get depleted. This final study is about learning to get out of the crisis mode.

THE BIG PICTURE

Take time to read this introduction with the group. There are some suggestions for how this can be done in the beginning of the leader's section.

A BIBLICAL PORTRAIT

Read Psalm 46

Question Three The psalmist is very honest about how turmoil and struggles can be a part of life. In the midst of the storm, we are called to find our refuge and strength in God. Only when we learn to walk with our God can we expect our lives to stay in balance. This is true for every area of life, including our marriage. When we let our lives spin out of control with business, insane schedules, and workaholism, it is easy for our priorities to get mixed up. There is no place left for stillness before our God. There is not room to grow as a follower of Christ. We need to honestly evaluate our lives and see what needs to be set aside so that we can have time to be still before God and also invest ourselves in a meaningful relationship with our spouse.

SHARPENING THE FOCUS

Read Snapshot "Pegged in the Red" before Question 4

Question Four There are a lot of consequences when you keep the RPMs in the red for too long. First, you tend to skim relationally. Your bond with your spouse that used to be strong and intimate becomes increasingly weak and distant. You hope he or she doesn't have a serious need because you don't have energy to deal with it. You hydroplane over conflicts. You put Band-Aids on serious problems. You resort to quick fixes and pretend things really aren't so bad.

You also skim with your kids. You don't keep track of them too well anymore. You no longer know what is going on in their lives. Little signs of trouble grab your attention, but you push them out of your mind. Warning flags wave, but you turn your head. You don't have the energy to face them—not now, anyway. Maybe tomorrow. Or maybe they will just go away.

Your friendships that used to be so deep and accountable are now characterized by shallowness. Your casual friendships don't even exist anymore. Pretty soon, nobody has access to you because you are so busy juggling and spinning.

You also skim in your relationship with God. You reduce your prayers to cries of desperation. You reduce worship to thanking God for helping you survive the madness of another week. You run too fast for reflection or meditation, for introspection or confession. You begin rationalizing little sins, and then bigger ones. Before you know it, you have journeyed far from spiritual innocence.

Then you start skimming emotionally. You find that your anger is flaring up more than it used to, but you don't take time to figure out why. You no longer pay attention to feelings like hurt or sadness or guilt. You become a mechanical soldier:

You just keep marching, doing what is necessary, and stuffing your feelings deeper and deeper inside. If you knew that those stuffed feelings were huddling together and planning an emotional insurrection that would one day scare the daylights out of you, you might pay attention to them. But you don't know that. Besides, you don't have the energy to go peeking under stones and trudging through the sticky muck of your emotional life. You don't have time to look inside.

Read Snapshot "A Shrinking Heart" before Question 5

Question Five I learned about a shrinking heart firsthand during the summer following the emotional crash described at the beginning of this session. Though I had begun to make some necessary life changes, I was still depleted emotionally when Lynne and the kids and I arrived in Michigan for our annual summer break.

The day after we arrived I talked with a friend in a local store. Just as we ended our conversation and I headed for the exit door, I noticed a Vietnam veteran in a motorized wheelchair whom I had seen around town the previous summer. He was leaving the store too, and arrived at the exit shortly ahead of me. While I waited impatiently for him to jockey his wheelchair through the narrow doorway, an unsettling awareness began churning inside me.

I sensed the Holy Spirit saying, "Take a look inside yourself right now, Bill. Isn't it true that you are more upset about the inconvenience of waiting thirty seconds to get out of this door than about the broken dreams this man carries around every day of his life? Isn't it true that your trivial inconvenience causes you more heartache than this man's tragedy?"

I walked to my car thinking, *What's wrong with me? I used to love people. I used to have compassion. I used to be moved by the lost, the needy, the hurting. Now all I care about is my convenience: "Don't bother me, pal. Get out of my way." I ought to be arrested!*

I spent the next four or five weeks replenishing myself emotionally. I separated myself from the pressures of ministry. I read for pleasure. I did fun, relaxing activities with my family. I enjoyed lighthearted conversations with close friends. I spent time alone.

One afternoon I was out running, and I saw that same Vietnam vet coming down the other side of the street in his wheelchair. When he was directly across the street from me I turned to look at him. Our eyes met, and it was like God gave me X-ray vision. I felt as if I were peering deep into his soul, and I began to cry over the heartbreak of his life. He was just about my age and had probably dreamed the same dreams and held the same aspirations that I had in my youth. But somewhere in a hostile jungle he had stepped on a land mine, and his whole life had come crashing in on him.

He turned and wheeled up a concrete ramp into a tiny clapboard cottage, and I was saddened to see him disappear. I wanted to reach out to him, talk to him, show him that I cared. I was filled with a swell of emotion.

While I continued my run, I thought about what had happened. I sensed the Holy Spirit saying, "You're on your way back, Bill. Your emotional tanks are filling, and you're starting to feel again. You're beginning to have compassion again."

Read Snapshot "Opt for a Slow Change" before Question 6

Question Seven Today's modern technology makes it possible for men and women to carry tremendous amounts of responsibility and to make every minute count. A pastor can conduct planning meetings on his car phone on the way to the airport, write sermons on his lap-top computer on the plane, speak in five cities in two days, and fax up-to-the-minute memos to his church staff. And that story is repeated in every other profession.

We finish one emotionally draining activity and have fifteen minutes before the next one starts. We run to the microwave, slide in a plate of pasta, and after thirty seconds, complain that "this thing takes forever!" The speed of our lives makes it impossible to recharge.

In Jesus' day, it may well have been easier to live a balanced life. Imagine that after speaking to a crowd in Jerusalem, Jesus decides to walk the fifteen or so miles to Jericho with his twelve disciples. They walk for a couple hours, then stop to cool off under a fig tree. They tell a few jokes, eat a few grapes, then slowly move on. A while later they pause at a well and chat with other travelers watering their camels, then they enjoy a drink themselves before hitting the road again. Before they know it, it's dinnertime, so they wander off the beaten path to gather wood for a fire. They quickly build a flaming pile of dry branches, but it takes some time for the coals to get hot. By the time dinner is done, it's dusk—no time to travel—so they settle in for the night, gathering round the roaring blaze to talk over the day.

I don't mean to minimize the rigors of first-century travel, but it's more than likely that something very healthy happened during those long hours of mundane activity. There was physical exercise, friendly conversation, long stretches of quiet for reflection and planning, and plenty of time for emotional reserves to trickle charge before the next draining demand.

Read Snapshot "Dare to Downshift" before Question 8

Question Eight In her cutting-edge book, *Downshifting* (HarperCollins), Amy Saltzman, an associate editor for *U. S. News & World Report*, describes the "gracious romantic porches" that adorn the homes on Newark Street in Washington, D.C. She calls them "tailor-made for reading Faulkner, chatting with the neighbors, watching the world go by." Yet she admits that during all her walks down Newark Street she had never seen anyone actually sitting on those enviably perfect porches. Successful young professionals dashed up and down the steps, but none had time to stop. That, Saltzman claims, "said it all" about the unhealthy pace of too many people's lives.

Saltzman suggests creative, practical ways for emotionally drained fast-trackers to "downshift" into more enjoyable patterns of life. People, she says, must redefine success in their own terms and live according to those new images.

"The new pictures in [downshifters'] heads are more eloquent, thoughtful and, ultimately, more satisfying. The front porch may not be as grand or the house it is attached to as large. But in this new picture, they are sitting on that porch, chatting with the neighbors, writing a letter to a friend and rereading that favorite old classic."

People living in crisis mode rarely sit on front porches and chat with neighbors. They rarely write letters to friends or reread favorite books. And, I might add, they rarely have warm, satisfying marriages.

What About You?

Of course, you may not be living in crisis mode. Maybe the threat of emotional depletion isn't your Achilles' heel. But unless you are a remarkable exception to the rule, you do have a weak spot. You do have an area of vulnerability.

Perhaps you have an uncontrollable temper fed by unresolved issues from your past or childhood memories that haunt you and make you withdraw from your spouse. Maybe you have low self-esteem that causes you to become unreasonably jealous or insecure. Perhaps you don't relate well to your parents and you take out your frustration on your spouse.

If this chapter does nothing else, we hope it will motivate you to discover your Achilles' heel, acknowledge the negative effect it has on you as an individual and as a marriage partner, and take steps to become healthy, whole, and strong.

We're not suggesting it will be easy or that changes can be made quickly. It took a solid year for me to make my journey back to wholeness. But at the end of that year, I felt like a different person. I had energy for life again. I was a contributor to my family again, and I was excited about my marriage again.

PUTTING YOURSELF IN THE PICTURE

Challenge group members to take time in the coming week to use part or all of this application section as an opportunity for continued growth.

ADDITIONAL WILLOW CREEK RESOURCES

Small Group Resources

Coaching Life-Changing Small Group Leaders, by Bill Donahue and Greg Bowman
The Complete Book of Questions, by Garry Poole
The Connecting Church, by Randy Frazee
Leading Life-Changing Small Groups, by Bill Donahue and the Willow Creek Team
The Seven Deadly Sins of Small Group Ministry, by Bill Donahue and Russ Robinson
Walking the Small Group Tightrope, by Bill Donahue and Russ Robinson

Evangelism Resources

Becoming a Contagious Christian (book), by Bill Hybels and Mark Mittelberg
The Case for a Creator, by Lee Strobel
The Case for Christ, by Lee Strobel
The Case for Faith, by Lee Strobel
Seeker Small Groups, by Garry Poole
The Three Habits of Highly Contagious Christians, by Garry Poole

Spiritual Gifts and Ministry

Network Revised (training course), by Bruce Bugbee and Don Cousins
The Volunteer Revolution, by Bill Hybels
What You Do Best in the Body of Christ—Revised, by Bruce Bugbee

Marriage and Parenting

Fit to Be Tied, by Bill and Lynne Hybels
Surviving a Spiritual Mismatch in Marriage, by Lee and Leslie Strobel

Ministry Resources

An Hour on Sunday, by Nancy Beach
Building a Church of Small Groups, by Bill Donahue and Russ Robinson
The Heart of the Artist, by Rory Noland
Making Your Children's Ministry the Best Hour of Every Kid's Week, by Sue Miller and David Staal
Thriving as an Artist in the Church, by Rory Noland

Curriculum

An Ordinary Day with Jesus, by John Ortberg and Ruth Haley Barton
Becoming a Contagious Christian (kit), by Mark Mittelberg, Lee Strobel, and Bill Hybels
Good Sense Budget Course, by Dick Towner, John Tofilon, and the Willow Creek Team
If You Want to Walk on Water, You've Got to Get Out of the Boat, by John Ortberg with Stephen and Amanda Sorenson
The Life You've Always Wanted, by John Ortberg with Stephen and Amanda Sorenson
The Old Testament Challenge, by John Ortberg with Kevin and Sherry Harney, Mindy Caliguire, and Judson Poling

WILLOW
Willow Creek Association

Willow Creek Association
Vision, Training, Resources for Prevailing Churches

This resource was created to serve you and to help you build a local church that prevails. It is just one of many ministry tools that are part of the Willow Creek Resources® line, published by the Willow Creek Association together with Zondervan.

The Willow Creek Association (WCA) was created in 1992 to serve a rapidly growing number of churches from across the denominational spectrum that are committed to helping unchurched people become fully devoted followers of Christ. Membership in the WCA now numbers over 10,500 Member Churches worldwide from more than ninety denominations.

The Willow Creek Association links like-minded Christian leaders with each other and with strategic vision, training, and resources in order to help them build prevailing churches designed to reach their redemptive potential. Here are some of the ways the WCA does that.

- **A2: Building Prevailing Acts 2 Churches—Today**—an annual two-and-a-half day event, held at Willow Creek Community Church in South Barrington, Illinois, to explore strategies for building churches that reach out to seekers and build believers, and to discover new innovations and breakthroughs from Acts 2 churches around the country.

- **The Leadership Summit**—a once a year, two-and-a-half-day conference to envision and equip Christians with leadership gifts and responsibilities. Presented live at Willow Creek as well as via satellite broadcast to over one hundred locations across North America, this event is designed to increase the leadership effectiveness of pastors, ministry staff, volunteer church leaders, and Christians in the marketplace.

- **Ministry-Specific Conferences**—throughout each year the WCA hosts a variety of conferences and training events—both at Willow Creek's main campus and offsite, across the U.S., and around the world—targeting church leaders and volunteers in ministry-specific areas such as: evangelism, small groups, preaching and teaching, the arts, children, students, women, volunteers, stewardship, raising up resources, etc.

- **Willow Creek Resources®**—provides churches with trusted and field-tested ministry resources in such areas as leadership, evangelism, spiritual formation, spiritual gifts, small groups, stewardship, student ministry, children's ministry, the use of the arts-drama, media, contemporary music —and more.

- **WCA Member Benefits**—includes substantial discounts to WCA training events, a 20 percent discount on all Willow Creek Resources®, *Defining Moments* monthly audio journal for leaders, quarterly *Willow* magazine, access to a Members-Only section on WillowNet, monthly communications, and more. Member Churches also receive special discounts and premier services through WCA's growing number of ministry partners—Select Service Providers—and save an average of $500 annually depending on the level of engagement.

For specific information about WCA conferences, resources, membership, and other ministry services contact:

Willow Creek Association
P.O. Box 3188
Barrington, IL 60011-3188
Phone: 847-570-9812
Fax: 847-765-5046
www.willowcreek.com

Continue building your new community!
New Community Series
BILL HYBELS AND JOHN ORTBERG
with Kevin and Sherry Harney

Exodus: *Journey Toward God* 0-310-22771-2

Parables: *Imagine Life God's Way* 0-310-22881-6

Sermon on the Mount[1]: *Connect with God* 0-310-22884-0

Sermon on the Mount[2]: *Connect with Others* 0-310-22883-2

Acts: *Build Community* 0-310-22770-4

Romans: *Find Freedom* 0-310-22765-8

Philippians: *Run the Race* 0-310-22766-6

Colossians: *Discover the New You* 0-310-22769-0

James: *Live Wisely* 0-310-22767-4

1 Peter: *Stand Strong* 0-310-22773-9

1 John: *Love Each Other* 0-310-22768-2

Revelation: *Experience God's Power* 0-310-22882-4

Look for New Community at your local Christian bookstore.

Continue the Transformation
Pursuing Spiritual Transformation
JOHN ORTBERG, LAURIE PEDERSON,
AND JUDSON POLING

Grace: *An Invitation to a Way of Life* 0-310-22074-2

Growth: *Training vs. Trying* 0-310-22075-0

Groups: *The Life-Giving Power of Community* 0-310-22076-9

Gifts: *The Joy of Serving God* 0-310-22077-7

Giving: *Unlocking the Heart of Good Stewardship* 0-310-22078-5

Fully Devoted: *Living Each Day in Jesus' Name* 0-310-22073-4

Look for Pursuing Spiritual Transformation at your local Christian bookstore.

TOUGH QUESTIONS
Garry Poole and Judson Poling

Softcover

REALITY CHECK SERIES
by Mark Ashton

Surviving a Spiritual Mismatch in Marriage

Lee Strobel and Leslie Strobel

Someone came between Lee and Leslie Strobel, threatening to shipwreck their marriage. No, it wasn't an old flame. It was Jesus Christ.

Leslie's decision to become a follower of Jesus brought heated opposition from her skeptical husband. They began to experience conflict over a variety of issues, from finances to child-rearing. But over time, Leslie learned how to survive a spiritual mismatch. Today they're both Christians— and they want you to know that there is hope if you're a Christian married to a nonbeliever. In their intensely personal and practical book, they reveal:

- Surprising insights into the thinking of non-Christian spouses
- A dozen steps toward making the most of your mismatched marriage
- Eight principles for reaching out to your partner with the gospel
- Advice for raising your children in a spiritually mismatched home
- How to pray for your spouse—plus a thirty-day guide to get you started
- What to do if you're both Christians but one lags behind spiritually
- Advice for single Christians to avoid the pain of a mismatch

Softcover: 0-310-22014-9
Abridged Audio Pages® Cassette: 0-310-22975-8

Pick up a copy today at your favorite bookstore!

ZONDERVAN™

GRAND RAPIDS, MICHIGAN 49530 USA

WWW.ZONDERVAN.COM

We want to hear from you. Please send your comments about this book to us in care of zreview@zondervan.com. Thank you.

ZONDERVAN™

GRAND RAPIDS, MICHIGAN 49530 USA

WWW.ZONDERVAN.COM